PUBLISHED by PARABLES
Earthly Stories with a Heavenly Meaning

The Christian Journey to Jesus Through Stories

By

Richard Gribble, CSC

Faith, Discipleship and Ministry: The Christian Journey to Jesus Through Stories
Richard Gribble CSC

Published By Parables
June, 2020

All Rights Reserved. No part of this book may be reproduced or utilized in any form or by any means, electronic or mechanical, including photocopying, recording, or by any information storage and retrieval system, without permission in writing from the author.

    ISBN 978-1-951497-69-9

    Printed in the United States of America

Readers should be aware that Internet Web sites offered as citations and/or sources for further information may have been changed or disappeared between the time this was written and the time it is read.

THE CHRISTIAN JOURNEY TO JESUS THROUGH STORIES

By

RICHARD GRIBBLE, CSC

PUBLISHED by PARABLES
Earthly Stories with a Heavenly Meaning

Dedication

Vocation, the response of each Christian to the call of God, is lived out day-by-day in varied ways. For most the vocation is to the married life and family, for some the single life, and for some others religious life and/or priesthood. While each and every vocation requires us to live lives of faith, discipleship, and ministry, my life as a religious priest in the Congregation of Holy Cross has been marked by many mentors and other significant religious and lay men and women who have shown me the proper road to Christ. It is appropriate, therefore, to dedicate this book to all those who have, through word and action, shown the face of Christ to me and allowed me to more fully live my own vocation of faith, discipleship, and ministry, most especially Sister Tania Santander Atauchi, CDP, whose inspiration to me over the last 18 years of her life was incalculable. This is the road that leads to Jesus, and one day to life eternal for all who believe.

The Christian Journey to Jesus Through Stories

Table of Contents

Introduction 7
Part I: Essays on Faith 11
Overview 13
Faith Brings Life 15
Place Your Trust in God 19
Don't Compromise Your Beliefs 23
All is Possible with God 27
Never Abandoned by God 31
The Path to God 37
Act on Your Faith 41
God Overcomes All Obstacles 47
Faith Conquers Fear 53
Trials of Faith 57
Encountering Christ, the Merciful One 61
Finding the Lost 67

Part II: Essays on Discipleship
71
Overview
73
The Challenge of Tough Love
75
Demonstrating God's Love to Others
79
Modeling the Faithfulness of God
83
Feeding Each Other
87
It's Never Too Late
91
Setting a "Straight" Example
95
Sharing the Message of Christ
99
Discipleship" Being All You Can Be
103
Discipleship Requires Commitment
107
Never Counting the Cost
111
Persistence Rewarded
117
If You Really Love me—Show Me!
121

Part III: Essays on Ministry 125
Overview 127
Completing the Master's Work 129
Be Ready for God's Call 133
Carrying Others' Burdens 137
Answering God's Call 141
Commitment to God and God's People 145
Carrying the Cross of Christ 149
Service: The Manifestations of God's Care 153
The Courage to Act 157
Responding to God's Call 161
Serve God Willingly 167
A Good Tree is Known by Its Fruits 173
The Hunger for Justice 179

Afterword 183

The Christian Journey to Jesus Through Stories

Introduction

G.K. Chesterton, the popular British writer and convert to Catholicism once famously wrote in *What's Wrong with the World* (1910), "The Christian ideal has not been tried and found wanting. It has been found difficult and left untried." Chesterton's words express both the privilege and the responsibility that are endemic to the Christian life. People throughout the world, but certainly those in a first world environment, enjoy many privileges. We enjoy the basic freedoms of constitutional democracy, such as life, liberty, and the pursuit of happiness as enshrined in the Declaration of Independence. Our day-to-day lives provide us with shelter, food and the other basic staples that have become normative in the post-modern world. We have the privilege of education and freedom of religious expression. But for those who profess Christ as Lord and Savior, undoubtedly the greatest privilege we have is our faith. We must recall that faith is indeed a gift granted to us by God. Jesus told his Apostles, "You did not choose me, but I chose you." (John 15:16) Indeed, the gift of faith, provided by God, was initially received by all through baptism. At that time Jesus, through the actions of the Church, chose us to be part of God's family. St. John reminds us, "See what love the Father has given us, that we should be called children of God; and that is what we are." He continues, "Beloved, we are God's children now; what we will be has not yet been revealed." (I John 3:1a, 2a)

The privileges we possess bring certain and at times significant responsibilities. As privileged citizens of a free land we have the responsibility to respond when our country calls. As individuals of significant education, it is our responsibility to help those with fewer opportunities. For all who bear the name Christian and possess the gift of faith, the responsibilities we have must be recognized and fulfilled. When we fail to meet our responsibilities in life, especially those tasks associated with civil society, the ramifications are generally swift and obvious. On the other hand, failure to meet our responsibilities that faith in Jesus

Christ requires will not land us in jail or find us ostracized from society. On the contrary in the contemporary 21st century world, such failures are so commonplace that one might actually be in the majority; no one would look askance at such failures.

Our responsibilities as Christians in the contemporary world are multiple and indeed a challenge, but unquestionably they must be engaged. With faith as our guardian and shield we must first take up the great responsibility of being disciples, followers of Jesus. Discipleship requires that we follow in the footsteps of the Master, listening to his words and following his example. In the contemporary world which has so many competing voices, all of which claim to point us in the proper direction, it is indeed difficult to hear the Word which is often drowned out by the cacophony of sounds that society generates. Listening to the words of Christ, therefore, requires that we concentrate, center our attention on him, and refuse to be swayed by voices that claim to hold solutions to the various problems and troublesome situations so commonplace today. Discipleship requires courage; it often necessitates us to take a path which is directly opposed to what society suggests is proper. Following Jesus requires us to take the less traveled path. Christ told us that this would be the case when he said, "Enter through the narrow gate; for the gate is wide and the road is easy that leads to destruction, and there are many who take it. For the gate is narrow and the road is hard that leads to life, and there are few who find it." (Matthew 7:13-14) Discipleship will also lead to suffering. Again, Jesus warned us, "If any want to become my followers, let them deny themselves and take up their cross and follow me. For those who want to save their life will lose it, and those who lose their life for my sake, and for the sake of the gospel, will save it". (Mark 8:34b-35) Yes, the road may be narrow and difficult and suffering will be our lot, but as St. Paul has written the goal we seek is worth the effort: "What no eye has seen, nor ear heard, nor the human heart conceived, what God has prepared for those who love him." (I Corinthians 2:9)

Initiating our discipleship, our walk with the Lord, is the first step in meeting our responsibilities as people of faith, but to sustain our relationship and move forward in the Christian life requires us to take the next step to active ministry. Just prior to his

Ascension, Jesus commissioned his apostles to go forth and do their share to complete the Master's work in the world: "Go therefore and make disciples of all nations, baptizing them in the name of the Father and of the Son and of the Holy Spirit, and teaching them to obey everything that I have commanded you." (Matthew 20:19-20a) Jesus started the Church and its work, but he left those who had walked in his steps, namely his disciples, in charge when he left this world to return to the Father. Clearly his expectation is that we will continue the mission, as best we are able with our God-given talents, the time we have, and the opportunities we are given. We are responsible to make the world a better place, not only the physical and technological environment in which we live, but a world that is more in tune with Christ's message of love and peace. If we don't take our responsibility to minister seriously, then the job simply will not get done. It is our task since Jesus is no longer physically present.

  This book, through the use of stories as a means to illustrate themes, presents a series of short reflective essays that illustrate, using Scripture as a base, a method to follow Jesus. Whether personally or in a group, reading one or two reflections per day, and taking a few moments to consider the challenge and respond to the questions can, it is hoped, be beneficial for one's spiritual growth. Reflections on faith encourage the reader to grasp the invitation extended by the Lord, to root oneself in the certainty that we are all children of God. Discipleship, the next step, requires us to actively seek to walk with the Lord in our daily lives. Passivity is not an option; rather we must follow the Master's lead and learn from him how to better serve others. With this knowledge we can then complete the cycle, by being active ministers in the church. We bring the message of Jesus with complete confidence that he is with us every step of the way. At the conclusion of the Great Commission described above, Jesus informs his disciples: "And remember, I am with you always, to the end of the age."

  The challenge of the Christian life, to be people of faith who walk as disciples in the footsteps of the Master and then minister in his name, has been succinctly and very powerfully articulated in a famous prayer by Saint Teresa of Avila: "Christ has nobody on earth that yours, no hands no feet but yours. Yours are the eyes with which Christ looks with compassion on the world. Christ has nobody on earth but yours." Yes, the great challenge for Christians today is to be Christ to others, to be his hands and feet, his eyes and ears in the world. It is my hope that this book of reflections can be a source of encouragement and challenge to help all who read it to persevere in their daily journey, to grow strong in faith, to walk closer to Jesus as his disciple and to be more active in ministry. The Lord Jesus is calling us; will we have the courage to respond?

          Richard Gribble, CSC

Part I: Essays on Faith

The Christian Journey to Jesus Through Stories

Overview

St. Anselm, the great British Benedictine monk left posterity what many consider the classic definition of theology: "Faith seeking understanding." Using Anselm's words, one can see that the study of God must begin with faith. But what is faith? Quite easily ten people could provide ten different, but all legitimate answers to this question. For me, however, the best definition is provided in the Letter to the Hebrews (11:1): "Now faith is the assurance of things hoped for, the conviction of things not seen." There are certainly many things in our lives that we hope to achieve, find, and accomplish; there are some equally if not more things that we hope will happen for family members, friends, and others we love. We certainly hope for good health, success in life--financially, professionally and personally--peace in our often-troubled world, and many other things, both personal and communal. But the author of the Letter to the Hebrews also says that faith is conviction, which is deeper and more profound than belief, about the things we cannot see. We have faith in God, the teachings of the Church and the future which we cannot know. Thus, faith is central to the life we live as Christians.

The centrality of faith for the Christian person makes it the foundation upon which the various aspects of our life must be built and eventually blossom. This foundation must be strong and secure. We recall Jesus' words on the need for a strong personal foundation:

> Everyone then who hears these words of mine and acts on them will be like a wise man who built his house on rock. The rain fell, the floods came, and the winds blew and beat on that house, but it did not fall, because it had been founded on rock. And everyone who hears these words of mine and does not act on them will be like a foolish man who built his house on sand. The rain fell, and the floods came and the winds blew and beat against the

> house, and it fell—and great was its fall. (Matthew 7:24-27)

Any structure, whether it be a physical building, an ideological concept, or a life of faith must be built upon a foundation that is strong and resistant to the outside forces that seek its destruction. Thus, the Christian journey, that is our day-to-day life, must be built on the rock foundation which is faith.

The essays in Part I address faith from various perspectives. We must learn not only the necessity of faith, but how to negotiate the various hurdles and obstacles that we often encounter in society that challenge our faith. We must realize that faith is not something we receive, and it remains a permanent part of us. Rather, faith must be continually strengthened and given the proper maintenance necessary for any foundation. If the base of a house, monument or even human ideal is severely damaged or not properly maintained, that which is built upon it will eventually crumble. Thus, in a similar way, faith must be a central concern in our daily life for without it our Christian vocation will be imperiled. Let us, therefore, continually build and strengthen our faith so that we can become true disciples of Jesus and minister to God's people in his name.

Faith Brings Life

It was a Sunday morning in South America, in a little chapel on the border of Venezuela and Colombia. As Mass was beginning, a not uncommon occurrence took place; a band of guerrillas armed with machine guns came out of the jungle and entered the chapel from a side door. The priest and the people were horrified and afraid. The men dragged the priest outside to be executed. The sound of gunfire was heard. The leader of the guerillas came back inside the chapel and shouted, "Anyone else who believes in this God stuff, come forward!" Everyone was petrified and thus they stood frozen; there was a long silence. Finally, one man came forward and stood in front of the guerrilla leader and said simply, "I love Jesus." He was roughed up, tossed to the soldiers, and taken outside for execution. Again, gunfire was heard. After more time several other members of the congregation came forward saying the same thing. They too were roughed up and escorted outside. The sound of machine gun fire was heard once again. When there were no others willing to identify themselves as Christians, the guerilla chief ordered all the members of the congregation outside. "You have no right to be here," he bellowed. Then the people were herded outside where they were astonished to see their pastor and the others standing there.

The priest and those who had confessed their faith in Jesus were ordered back into the chapel to continue the Mass, but the others were angrily told to stay out. "Until," said the guerilla chief, "you have the courage to stand up for your beliefs and be committed, you have no right to worship." And with that the guerillas disappeared into the jungle.

This apocryphal, yet highly illustrative story, suggests that if one possesses sufficient faith and is willing to stand up for what one believes that, in the end, life will be the reward. In a similar way, Scripture shows that faith brings life, for our God is not a God of death, but one who brings us life today and eternal life tomorrow.

The story in Mark's Gospel of the cure of the women with the hemorrhage and Jairus' daughter (5:21-43) is very purposely presented in a very structured way to highlight the need for faith. The story of the woman is "framed," by the story of Jairus' daughter. Mark uses this technique, namely using the girl's story as a set of bookends, to emphasize the great faith of the woman and Jairus. Both firmly believe that Jesus can bring healing. Jairus asks Jesus to lay his hands on his daughter; the woman believes that if she touches the Lord she will be restored to health. In each case, because of their strong faith, in spite of all the odds and regardless of what others might think or do, they act by invoking the Lord. They are convinced that if they stay the course, all will be well. While a different set of circumstances, the faithful in the jungle chapel, held the same faith.

Clearly all three, those in the jungle chapel, Jairus and the woman most assuredly believed that God was a God of life. The author of the Book of Wisdom (1:13-14a) makes this abundantly clear: "For he created all things so that they might exist; the generative forces of the world are wholesome, and there is no destructive poison in them." God does not rejoice in death or destruction. Rather God fashioned humanity to be indestructible, namely God made us to share eternal life with him. Those who possess God will experience life. God desires life for all. Similarly, we remember how the Lord instructed Moses and the Israelites in the desert to "Choose life." (Deuteronomy 30:19) Clearly, we must also choose life, for ourselves and others. We do so by manifesting the faith that God has planted deep in our beings.

The contemporary highly secularized world in which we live is, unfortunately, almost antithetical to the practice of faith in God and the life which comes from it. Life tosses us plenty of curves and at times it is difficult to continue to stand in the batter's box and wait for the next pitch. We are wary; experience tells us that there are many alternatives to faith in God as the solutions to the problems and situations that at times vex us. We look to the world and all its allurements; we find solace and comfort by escaping from the world. We at times believe that the human resolution will be the cure. All of these possibilities, however, are only band-aids; they will neither heal our wounded and broken condition nor direct us toward the proper path that leads to God and, therefore, life.

Those parishioners in the jungle chapel, as well as Jairus and the woman with the hemorrhage, were forced to make a decision: Did they have sufficient faith in Jesus to know in their hearts that he and he alone could bring life? Let us rise above the secular solution and seek always the divine response. Let us place our faith in Jesus, allow Christ to be the one to whom we turn, with total confidence, believing that he will bring us life today and even more importantly, eternal life tomorrow!

Questions to Ponder:

1. When adversity strikes, how has my faith challenged me to respond?
2. Where do I go when the dilemmas and eventual obstacles of life seek to overwhelm me?
3. How have I challenged others to exercise their faith in the face of adversity, in its many manifestations?
4. How have I manifested recently the basic Church teaching on the sanctity of life?
5. What more must I do to place absolute trust and confidence in God, knowing that God is at my side every moment of every day?

Place Your Trust in God

He came silently, unobserved, yet strange to say, everyone recognized him. The time was the 15th century; the place was Seville in Spain. He came to bring peace; he came to bear witness to the truth. In short, he came to revive the commitment all men and women must make in placing their lives completely in God's hands. As he walked through the city he came upon the main square. A funeral procession was just beginning to form in front of the cathedral. A young girl had died the previous day. Moved with pity he came upon the scene. He heard the sobs and saw the tears of the girl's mother. As he approached, the bearers of the coffin halted. He touched the girl; he prayed for a minute. The girl was restored to full health and life. He returned the child to her mother.

The Cardinal Archbishop of Seville heard about this display of power, this show of trust. Such behavior was not to be tolerated; it only led to false hopes on the part of the people. Thus, the visitor was thrown into prison like a common criminal. He was to be interrogated, not by just any person, but by the one person whose presence in the city was the true symbol of Church orthodoxy, the chief or Grand Inquisitor of the Spanish Inquisition. The Inquisitor began his questioning of the prisoner. "Why have you returned? You can see that we no longer need you!" The prisoner only answered with silence. The Inquisitor continued his harangue. He questioned the prisoner about his time in the desert when he had been tempted by Satan: "You were a fool; you could have had it all. Satan offered you power, wealth, and prestige, but you chose miracle, mystery, love, and trust instead." Again, the prisoner only answered with silence. Finally, the Inquisitor, exasperated at the prisoner, rebuked him, "We no longer need what you can offer us. Go and leave us!" This time the prisoner answered, not with words but with action. He stood up, embraced the Inquisitor, kissed him, and then walked out of the prison, to another people in another time.

Fydor Dostoyevsky's classic tale "The Grand Inquisitor" told in his equally classic and famous novel *The Brothers Karamazov*, is a negative account of Christ's rejection by people upon his return to earth. Scripture illustrates this same message, both directly and, as one might say, "through the backdoor." We must listen to this message and apply it in our daily lives.

The prophet Zephaniah writes to the Hebrew people before their exile to Babylon. Zephaniah foresees the day of the exile, what he calls the day of God's wrath. The people have placed all their trust and hope in their own worldly pursuits and efforts. They have forgotten about God; there is no longer a need to trust in God. Thus, the prophet exhorts the people to live lives of greater humility, lives of greater justice. He writes, "Seek the Lord, all you humble of the land, who do his commands; seek righteousness, seek humility." (Zephaniah 2:3a) Those who refuse to place their trust in God will be carried off to exile. There will be, however, a remnant, those who have placed their hope in God, who will remain, as a sign of God's faithfulness.

In a similar way, St. Paul writes to the Christian community at Corinth, a people who were very special to him. If contemporary Scripture scholars are correct and II Corinthians is really a compilation of five or six letters which Paul wrote, then we actually have six or seven letters to the community, instead of the two recognized canonical letters. Moreover, Paul lived with this community for long stretches of time, as the Acts of the Apostles tells us. Knowing this, it is especially significant when Paul says to this community (1:31a) "Let the one who boasts, boast in the Lord." Those who think themselves important or of high rank will be shamed by those who are weak, the seemingly unimportant, the low born. God sends people into our lives who will keep us from getting too puffed up, from placing our complete trust in the things of this world. These people will show us that the path to life can only be through the ways of God.

Jesus strongly emphasizes this important Christian virtue in the Beatitudes, the beginning of his famous Sermon on the Mount. These beautiful words present a list of those who have been able to place their complete confidence and trust in God. Moreover, Jesus also tells us what the reward will be for each group who can trust

God. Jesus is saying in essence that we need to be content with the life God has given to us. Jesus is not saying that it is good to be sorrowing, to be hungry or thirsty. He is not saying that it is a good thing to suffer persecution. But he is saying that if we find ourselves in such a position, can we then place our trust in God to find solutions. Jesus is saying that we certainly must do all that we can to better our lot, but in the end, we must be content with the life God has given to us.

It is not the 15th century in Spain. It is the 21st century in the United States. I wonder if things have really changed that much. We live in a society, which we all know is not content or satisfied with the solutions of God. Such solutions are intangible; they are usually not immediate. What is especially frustrating for most people is that the solutions of God give us no control. Jesus asks us to cast aside all and to trust in him, for at times we will all find ourselves in some if not all of the Gospel beatitudes. Sometimes we will be full of sorrow; sometimes we will hunger for God. Sometimes we will be persecuted. When we find ourselves in these situations how do we react? Do we seek only the material, the human solution or can we place our trust in God? Do we become angry when life places us in a position we would rather not endure, or can we find the presence of Christ and share that with others no matter what the circumstances of our life may be? When we find ourselves in one of the categories of the beatitudes do we throw in the towel, give up and say that life is no longer worth living or do we continue to push forward and fully believe that our lives, when in God's hands, will, in the end find, the place that we ultimately seek? In short can we place sufficient trust in God and believe as St. Paul suggests that Jesus must be our wisdom, our justice, our sanctification, and our redemption?

Christ challenges us every day to place greater trust in God. We must listen to the author of the Book of Proverbs (3:5) who writes, "Trust in the Lord will all your heart, on your own intelligence rely not." Let us take up the challenge of Scripture and be converted to a greater sense of trust in God. Let us pick up our cross, walk the road, seek God, and in the process find eternal life as well.

Questions to Ponder:

1. How do I manifest my trust in the Lord? Can others "see" that I am a disciple of Jesus Christ?
2. How accepting am I to the presence of the Lord in my life? Do I believe I can "go it alone?"
3. How does the attraction of the material world find a place in my thinking?
4. How does pride enter into my daily life? How does pride compete with God?
5. How have I reacted when God's solution to a problem is not mine?

Don't Compromise Your Beliefs

William Jennings Bryan was a man of great conviction who never compromised his beliefs regardless of their cost. He was born in Illinois in the mid-nineteenth century but came to national prominence as a Congressman from Nebraska. In 1896, on the floor of the House of Representatives, Bryan gave an electrifying address, known as his "Cross of Gold Speech," which supported bimetallism, the idea of placing the United States on a silver as well as a gold standard. This concept was very popular among the Populists, an agrarian movement of the latter nineteenth century that supported farmers and those with little or no voice in American society. Bryan was one of their champions. The speech and his public presence impressed the Democrats so much that Party officials asked Bryan to be their candidate for President at the tender age of 36, only one year above the minimum age to hold the nation's highest office.

Bryan was defeated in the 1896 election by William McKinley, but that did not stop his advocacy for others. He became a popular newspaper editor and he continued to champion the underdog in American society. In 1900 the Democrats again asked him to run for President, but he lost a second time. In 1908 Bryan was again nominated and lost a third time, but he was not a man who would compromise his beliefs to win an election. His uncompromising attitude manifest itself in 1917 when, as Secretary of State in the administration of Woodrow Wilson, he resigned his high office when the United States entered World War I, believing the war to be immoral.

Undoubtedly, the event for which William Jennings Bryan will be most remembered, however, was the last hurrah of his life. In 1925 Bryan was the prosecuting attorney in the famous John Scopes "Monkey Trial" in Dayton, Tennessee. Scopes, a high school biology teacher, had intentionally broken a new state ordinance which forbade the teaching of Charles Darwin's theory of evolution in Tennessee's public schools. Bryan, a man of deep

Christian faith as well as a famous politician, was asked by the Fundamentalist lobby to be their champion and defend creationism and the inerrancy of the Bible. Bryan's opponent was the famous Chicago jurist, Clarence Darrow. The story of this famous trial is captured in the popular stage play and movie, "Inherit the Wind." Although Bryan was berated by Darrow on the stand for his beliefs, he held fast. In the end the prosecution won; Bryan had championed his last cause for only days after the trial ended, he died of a heart attack. William Jennings Bryan, a man of true conviction, never counted the cost of discipleship and refused to compromise his beliefs.

The life and career of William Jennings Bryan is an excellent example of an important theme in the Scriptures, namely that as men and women of faith, we must be willing to stand up for what we believe and refuse to compromise our values. Jeremiah, like several of the Old Testament prophets, did not want the job that God gave him. Yet, despite the personal cost, he went forward and proclaimed God's message to an often-rebellious people. In 20:10-13, the prophet speaks of a plot hatched against him. People cry, "Denounce him! Let us denounce him!" The prophet responds, "All my close friends are watching for me to stumble." (Jeremiah 20:10b) Jeremiah knows that his life is in jeopardy, but he is equally confident that God is with him, to be his mighty champion. God will not allow others to triumph, but rather will put them to shame. Jeremiah has entrusted his life and cause to God and the Lord will respond.

In Matthew's Gospel (10:26-33) Jesus says that we can confidently go forward and do whatever it is that God asks of us, because the Father is always watching over us. We read, "Do not fear those who kill the body but cannot kill the soul; rather fear him who can destroy both soul and body in hell. ...So do not be afraid." (Matthew 10:28, 31a) Anyone who acknowledges the Father will not be forgotten.

If we need further evidence of the manifold and manifest presence of God in our life, who will direct us along straight and proper paths, we need to hear what St. Paul writes to the Romans (5:12-15) in one of the most famous passages in the whole Pauline corpus. The apostle says that as through one man, that is Adam, sin entered the world and with sin death, so also through obedience of one man, namely Jesus, we have been saved. We did nothing to earn this great gift; it is the desire of God who created us that we be with him forever. Thus, Jesus was sent to heal what was damaged and to bring us home.

    The message of the life of William Jennings Bryan and Scripture is crystal clear--but are we listening? Too often, usually because society says it is the "proper" way to go, we choose the uncluttered and more frequently walked path, the way that is easier. Why would one consider the way that might bring pain, problems, or aggravation? We often compromise who we are and what we believe for expediency, acceptance, and simply to avoid hassles and possibly the ire of another. When was the last time when we found ourselves in a discussion about some controversial issue, such as the life and death issue of abortion, euthanasia, and the death penalty that we had the courage to present the Church's teaching and stand behind it? Often, we find ourselves swept away by powerful and influential people to engage in unethical business practices and similar inappropriate conduct in order to save money, make the company appear better off than it is, or create the proper impression? We must develop the strength, courage, and faith of people like William Jennings Bryan and the Prophet Jeremiah and realize that Jesus' message is true--God will never forget us. God will give us the strength, courage, and faith to hold our values if we will only give him the opportunity to show us.

    Let us be confident of God's presence in our lives; let us believe that the hairs of our head are counted by God. Let us recall what Jesus says toward the end of his famous Sermon on the Mount (Matthew 7:13-14), "Enter through the narrow gate, for the gate is wide and the road easy that leads to destruction, and there are many who take it. For the gate is narrow and the road is hard that leads to life, and there are few who find it," Let us choose the narrow path, the path of William Jennings Bryan, the path of Jeremiah and St. Paul, the one and only path that will bring us to eternal life.

Questions to Ponder:

1. Why do I at times compromise the beliefs that Christians consider central to the faith?
2. How do I react when others turn their back on me because of the things I say and the beliefs I hold? Do I maintain the courage of my convictions during such challenging times?
3. How have I responded to the call of Jesus to stand with him against the "tidal wave" of contemporary secularism and religious indifference?
4. Why do I too often choose the easy and uncluttered path of life, when I know the narrow gate in the only route to eternal life?
5. How have I manifested my gratitude to Jesus for his great sacrifice in dying for me?

All Is Possible with Faith

They said it could never be done. They said it was humanly impossible to run a mile under four minutes. The world record in the mile run, 4:01.4, had been set in 1945; nobody had seriously challenged it. But on May 7, 1954, Roger Bannister proved the world to be wrong!

Roger Bannister had been running all his life. Born and raised in England, Roger ran to avoid those who told him his dreams were impossible. Coming from a poor family, people told him it would be impossible to study medicine; the money was not present for such a dream. Coming from a lesser-educated family, people said it would be impossible to gain entrance to a reputable university; he had no contacts or references. But medical student Roger Bannister of Oxford University proved everyone wrong.

Possessing a bright mind and physical prowess Bannister began to study the mechanics of running. His study helped him to perfect his style on the track; he was able to run faster. His study also helped him to overcome all who constantly said, "No, it can't be done." On that cold and windy day in May, however, Roger Bannister made history. In a rather obscure and unpublicized meet Roger crossed the finish line in the mile run in 3:59.4 seconds. He was the first human to ever run the mile in less than four minutes; the impossible was made possible.

The story of Roger Bannister is one of many examples with which we are all familiar that says with faith and confidence we can do anything. The Bible describes how with faith in God all things become possible. In Matthew's Gospel (14:22-33) Jesus contrasts one whose faith is absolute and one whose faith falters. Jesus is, as would be expected, the one whose faith is absolute. Jesus walks on the water; he calms the storm on the lake. Jesus has demonstrated his divinity for only God can do what Jesus does. The disciples recognize Jesus as Lord when he enters the boat, "Surely you are the Son of God." Jesus has demonstrated that he is

God, but he has also shown the absolute faith which he possesses in the Father's presence in him as well.

Peter, the leader of the apostles, yet the disciple in Scripture who shows the greatest humanity through his brokenness, is the one whose faith falters. He begins to walk on the water at Jesus' invitation. But opposition enters through the presence of the strong wind and waves. Peter's faith is challenged; he wavers and begins to sink. Jesus rescues him but also reprimands his chosen leader, "Why did you doubt?" (14:31b) In short, Jesus is asking, can't you believe that with trust, faith and confidence all is possible?

The First Book of Kings (19:9-13) provides another story of faith. Elijah, the man of God, believes that God will be made manifest; God can come in many ways. He is told to go to the mouth of the cave and wait, for the Lord will pass-by. Elijah believed that certainly God could be present in the power of an earthquake or fire. But he also believed that that God could be present in the gentleness of a soft whispering sound. Elijah discounts nothing; all is possible with God.

We need to be like Elijah and have his sense of trust and faith. How much trust do we or can we place in the presence of God in our lives? Can we walk into uncertainty like Peter walked on the water? Can we trust that God will be with us in our efforts? Can we believe that nothing is impossible with the help of our God?

We gather at Mass each Sunday, an act which in itself demonstrates our faith and trust. We come to Mass with the belief that the bread and wine become the Body and Blood of Christ. Our belief in such an action is impossible without faith. If we can believe in something so seemingly impossible as the Eucharist, then why do we lose faith in God's presence and action in our world? Let us also strive to show faith in God's presence and, thereby, become more God-like in our actions and attitudes. With such an attitude, we like Dr. Roger Bannister can profess in confidence, that with God's help the difficult we do today and the impossible we will do tomorrow.

Questions to Ponder:

1. What holds me back from believing that with God all thigs are possible?
2. What challenges my faith to believe that God is present in all things and at all times?
3. How do I see the face and presence of God in others, especially those I find difficult or troublesome?
4. Realizing that I am broken and incomplete, like Peter, what can I do to make my relationship with the Lord stronger?
5. When Jesus asks me to do what I believe is impossible, like walking on water, how have I responded?

The Christian Journey to Jesus Through Stories

Never Abandoned by God

The priest and popular author, Joseph Girzone, tells the following story in his parable *Joshua and the Children*. Over a hundred years ago in France, a wealthy family lived in Paris. Because of their means the family employed a butler. This butler, who was young and greedy, concocted a plot to steal the family fortune, hidden in a vault in their home. In order to complete his plan without getting caught, the butler believed he needed to kill all the members of the family. Thus, late one evening the butler entered the family home and methodically began to murder all the people in the house. He went to the master bedroom and killed the parents first. Then one by one he began to murder the children. The youngest escaped because he heard noises and could not sleep. When he realized what was happening, he quietly slipped out of his bedroom and hid in a closet under a pile of dirty clothes. The butler never found him.

For some time, the boy wandered the streets as an orphan, but he was eventually taken in by a kind priest and raised as if he were his own son. He eventually entered the seminary and became a priest himself. After serving in a couple of parishes, he was assigned by the archbishop to Devil's Island, the French penal colony, as a chaplain.

One afternoon, after having been on the Island for about six months, the chaplain was in his office. Suddenly one of the inmates came running in from the fields, frantically calling for the priest: "There is a man dying out in the field, Father, come quickly." The priest ran out with the inmate and reached the dying prisoner. Kneeling down beside him, the priest lifted the man's head onto his lap and asked if he would like to confess his sins. The dying man refused. "Why not my son?" asked the priest. "Because God will never forgive me for what I have done," came the response. "But what have you done that is so bad?" the priest continued. The old man went on to tell the story of how when he was young, he was serving as a butler for a rich Parisian family and how he had killed this whole family so that he could steal their money. Only the youngest boy escaped because he could not find him. Then the priest, with tears in his eyes, said to the dying man, "If I can forgive you, then certainly God can forgive you. And I forgive you from my heart. It was my family you killed, and I am that little boy."

The convict cried and told the priest how he had been haunted all his life over what he had done, though no one else knew about it. Even the authorities never found out. The two men cried together and as the priest was giving the dying man absolution, the prisoner died with his head resting on the priest's lap.

This powerful story speaks clearly of the great compassion and love which God has for us, no matter what has happened or when it occurred. God will provide the opportunity to release ourselves from the bondage that sin can sometimes bring to our lives. Scripture often speaks of the magnanimous forgiveness and compassion of God for all people.

The prophecy of Isaiah is actually three books in one, God's word spoken to the prophet before, during, and after the infamous Babylonian Exile. In Isaiah 43:18-25, which is found in the middle section, we realize that the people had transgressed God's law, the Covenant, many times; that is why they were sent into exile. Some of the people might have thought that God had abandoned them, that the Lord would never be able to forgive them for what they had done. Yet, the Lord says, through the words of Isaiah, "Do not remember the former things or consider the things of old, I am about to do a new thing." (43:18) He uses the beautiful image of a new spring, a source of water that will come forth in the desert. The people may feel burdened with their sins and wearied with their crimes, but God wipes away all sin; it is remembered no more.

St. Paul takes this idea and moves it one important step further in writing to the Corinthians. He writes, "As surely as God is faithful, our word to you has not been Yes and No. For the Son of God, Jesus Christ … was not yes and no; but in him is always yes." (II Corinthians 1:18-19) Paul says that God is ever faithful. God is not sometimes yes and other times no; God is never anything but yes. There is nothing negative about God. God is the one who establishes us, anoints us, and seals us. God is present in every aspect of life.

God's ever present nature is rather dramatically depicted in the Gospel of Mark (2:1-12) In this pericope Jesus is impressed with the faith of the friends of a paralytic who, unable to bring the latter to Jesus, open the roof above his head and lower him down so that Jesus may cure him. Through his action, Jesus teaches the scribes and others who witness this miracle an important lesson that God cannot be separated from any part of our lives. God heals; God forgives; God is ever present. God will never abandon us!

We need to learn the lesson taught by the priest and God, the lesson learned by the prisoner and the Hebrews. We must learn and hold as our conviction through faith that God is ever present, and that God forgives. God does not hold grudges; God will never abandon us.

We might think that we are weak, that we are sinners and unable to approach God. If we believe that we are incomplete then we are correct, for indeed we are imperfect. However, God knows this fact better than we do, for this is precisely the way God made us. Since we were created in an incomplete state, God has provided a way for us to become more complete. That vehicle is reconciliation, a process that must begin with our confident knowledge that God is present to us in every possible way. Some people today, like the Hebrews in an earlier time, believe that God has abandoned us, that there is something they have done that cannot be forgiven by God. This, however, is totally impossible. We must recall the words of God as echoed by the prophet, "Can a woman forget her nursing child, or show no compassion for the child of her womb? Even these may forget, yet I will not forget you." (Isaiah 49:15)

Yes, it is true--God is ever present, holds no grudges, and forgives us completely. If we believe this is the way God acts toward us, should we not try and emulate these virtues in our lives, especially in our relationship with God and God's people? Many of us carry around old grudges, past hurts, insults, and failures. We will not let them go. Some still believe that God cannot forgive them some transgression of the past. With these burdens we live in a state of alienation and isolation. We are alienated from others and we isolate ourselves from God's love. We live as if there was a ball and chain tied around our leg. It slows us down; at times it may even stop us dead in our tracks. Jesus today suggests that we need to cut the chain and let the past go.

We need to move forward to the fresh spring of new life which the Lord can give to us. The priest was able to cut the chain of pain and suffering that the old man carried for so many years. God cut the chain of sin that kept the Hebrews bound up and offered them a new life. Jesus cured the paralytic, not only in body but in spirit. Let us be free and know that God will not abandon us. Let us turn toward Jesus, the one who is always yes, the one who unties us and sets us free, the one who brings us to eternal life.

Questions to Ponder:

1. Why do I at times give up on others or on God, knowing that the Lord is with me at every moment of every day?
2. Why is offering forgiveness to others so difficult for me?
3. What past painful experiences prevent me from being the person God intended me to be?
4. What methods have I developed and/or used that equip me better to be a person who offers forgiveness to others?
5. Who best presents Jesus' model of forgiveness to me?

The Path to God

The resident bishop at the Cathedral of Notre Dame in Paris, who was known to be a great evangelist, reaching out to cynics, unbelievers, and scoffers, told the following story. It seems that years ago there was a young man who would daily stand outside the cathedral and shout terrible words and derogatory slogans against God, the Church, and anyone who entered the cathedral. He would call these people fools and all sorts of other names. People tried to ignore the man, but it was rather difficult.

One day the priest rector of the cathedral went outside to confront the man. The young man ranted and raved against everything the priest told him. Finally, the priest addressed the young man. "Look," he said, "let's get this over with once and for all. I am going to dare you to do something and I bet you cannot do it." "Of course," the young man, gruffly responded, "I can do anything you propose." "Fine," said the priest. "All that I ask is that you come with me into the church and follow me into the sanctuary. I want you to stare at the figure of Christ and I want you to scream at the top of your lungs, as loudly as you can, 'Christ died on the cross for me and I don't care a bit.'" So, the young man entered the sanctuary and screamed as loud as he could, while looking at the figure on the cross, "Christ died on the cross for me and I don't care a bit." The priest said, "Very good. Now do it again." And again, the man screamed, "Christ died on the cross for me and I don't care a bit." "You're almost done now, said the priest. One more time."

The main raised his fist, kept looking at the statue, but the words would not come out. He just could not look at the face of Christ and say the words anymore. Then, the bishop, to the surprise of all said, "I was that young man. That defiant young man was me. I thought that I didn't need God but found that I did."

This story is apocryphal, but it is nonetheless a good illustration of how God works in our lives, transforming our hearts, even when we might not want such transformation, to the realization that we cannot live our lives without God. Scripture describes how God works in our lives, even we don't want it, providing us with the sustenance we need to do what God asks of us.

Elijah (I Kings 19:4-8) found himself in the desert and he waited expectantly for death. God, however, had other plans for this great prophet. God needed Elijah to continue his ministry, but he needed him to do so from the mountain of God, Horeb, which was a great distance away. Thus, not once but twice God interceded in Elijah's life, sending an angel who provided food and water so that he would have the requisite energy for the journey. Strengthened by the nourishment that God provides, the prophet walked forty days and forty nights to Horeb, sometimes called Sinai, where Moses had received the Law, what Christians call the Ten Commandments.

Many times the people Jesus encountered were rather incredulous; they did not want to believe or to listen to what the Lord said. John chapter 6 includes what Scripture scholars call "the Bread of Life discourse." Jesus claims, "I am the bread of life. Whoever comes to me will never be hungry, and whoever believes in me will never be thirsty." (6:35) In essence Jesus is saying that the people cannot live without him. Like the angry young man who denounced God and the Church, many of Jesus' listeners cannot understand their need for God. Yet, Jesus is very clear that only those who believe, only those who participate with and remain close to him will ever find eternal life.

Our very complex and fast-paced contemporary society is not the environment that is often conducive to the proper path of life. St. Paul understood this, even writing to people 2000 years ago. Ephesus, in Paul's time, was a commercial center where trade, idolatry, and the hustle and bustle of society estranged people from God. Thus, he writes to the Christian community there and tells them they need to change their attitudes and many of the practices of their lives. We read, "Put away from you all bitterness and wrath and anger and wrangling and slander, together with all malice, and be kind to one another, tenderhearted, forgiving one another, as God in Christ has forgiven you. (Ephesians 4: 31-32) Succinctly put, Paul tells the people to imitate God and follow his path of love.

Few people are like the angry young man and want to stand outside a church and bad mouth God and the Church. However, unfortunately, most of us, sometimes consciously but many times unconsciously, live our lives as if we do not need God. We rely on the people and things of the world for all the answers we seek to problems and the various questions of daily life. We feel we can go it alone; who needs God to accomplish great things in this life? Then, something happens and we, like the angry man who became the bishop, like Elijah, are humbled sufficiently to realize our absolute need for God. Even if we conquer the world, earn a million dollars, or find recognition in every aspect of society, if we don't have God, we will not attain the one and only goal that has lasting meaning, namely eternal life.

Therefore, let us learn an important lesson from the Bishop's story and Scripture, and realize our need to always seek and walk the path of God. It is the one and only path to salvation and eternal life.

Questions to Ponder:

1. How do I, often unknowingly, show that I don't need God in my life?
2. When was the last time I felt anger toward God? How did I get back on the right track?
3. Why at times do I not believe that with God all things are indeed possible?
4. What actions and attitudes need to be rooted out of my life, so I will live more consistent with Jesus' message of love?
5. When things don't work out as I anticipate what has been my reaction? How do I deal with adversity?

Act on Your Faith

The Great Depression was undoubtedly one of the darkest hours in American history. Beginning with the great stock market crash of October 1929, the nation almost overnight found itself in an economic death spiral of unparalleled magnitude. Fortunes accumulated during the halcyon days of "the roaring twenties" were lost, people were thrown out of work and despair gained the upper hand in the minds of the individual American where confidence had earlier reigned supreme.

The need for action had never been greater and all eyes turned to Washington, D.C. and the President, Herbert Hoover, for answers. Hoover was a champion of American individualism. For him compassion was understood as it had traditionally been known for decades in the United States--people helped each other. Families, communities, and fraternal orders met the needs. Financial bailout was not the responsibility of the Federal Government. But as much a Hoover believed in this ideology, the nation's economic status and with it the plight of the individual worker only grew worse.

In March 1933 a new President, Franklin Delano Roosevelt, came to the White House and he gave the American people fresh hope through what he called the "New Deal." Roosevelt believed the government could not hide behind tradition and say, "It has always been done this way," as did his predecessor, but that unique difficulties required new and special solutions. Thus, Roosevelt at rapid pace, in his famous first "100 days," introduced and was able to convince Congress to pass a whole series of initiatives that were geared toward restoring economic prosperity and human pride by getting people back to work and relieving the daily suffering that the prolonged Depression had created. The New Deal was an alphabet soup of agencies and government offices that initiated the recovery that was needed. The National Industrial Recovery Act (NIRA) was the basic program. Under this umbrella was the Agricultural

Adjustment Act (AAA) to aid farmers, the Federal Emergency Relief Administration (FERA) to meet immediate needs of the poor and unemployed, and the Public Works Administration (PWA) and Works Progress Administration (WPA) which were designed to get people back to work on a government subsidy.

President Roosevelt was not content to hide behind "what had always been done," but boldly went forward and acted. He did what needed to be done, as innovative as it was. He saw a need and took action. While people may argue historically about FDR, he was unquestionably a man of action, who did what was necessary and was not concerned with precedence.

The inauguration of Franklin Roosevelt's New Deal is a good example of one of the central teachings of Jesus, namely that we cannot hide behind laws and preset ways of doing things, but must act on God's word as it comes to us and do what is necessary to meet the needs of God's people.

The Torah or sacred Jewish Scripture, the first five books of the Old Testament, is absolutely fundamental to the understanding of this first great Western religious tradition. In the Book of Deuteronomy, Moses speaks to the Israelites about the centrality of the Law. What became known as the Mosaic Law was the rock upon which the people based their lives. Nothing was more important. Moses tells the people, "You must neither add anything to what I command you nor take anything from it but keep the commandments of the Lord your God with which I am charging you. "(Deuteronomy 4:2) The people are to observe the precepts of the Law with great care.

The centrality of the Law continued into the time of Jesus, who, as we know, was a good practicing Jew. But the Lord brought a fresh perspective, viewing the Law as an aide to finding God, not as a series of proscriptions. He tells the Pharisees and experts in the Law that they have used the Law as a shield to keep them from doing what is more important. The Jewish religious leaders were guilty of hiding behind the Law as an excuse for disregarding the needs of the poor and others who needed their assistance. It was very comfortable for the Pharisees to observe the outward dictates of the Law, but they failed to go the next step and think of others. Thus, Jesus added the spirit of the Law when he proclaimed, "Do not think I have come to abolish the law or the prophets; I have come not to abolish but to fulfill." (Matthew 5:17)

In a similar way, St. James makes it very clear what is necessary if we are to follow the path of Jesus. We read, "In fulfillment of his own purpose he gave us birth by the word of truth, so that we would become a kind of first fruits of his creatures." (James 1:18) He goes on to say in essence that we must welcome the word and act upon it. If all we do is listen, we are deceiving ourselves. The deception of the Jewish religious leaders was that they were content to adhere to the letter of the Law without acting upon it. Similarly, Herbert Hoover, while I am sure well intentioned, was content to do what others before him had done; he too was unwilling to act.

We live in an action-oriented society, but unfortunately most of the things we do are for ourselves and not for the common good. We are not willing to go the extra mile and think of innovative ways in which we can serve and assist. We say, I have always done it that way, why should I change now? I don't have the time nor the energy necessary to do something different. There are times as well that we hide behind other people, rules, tradition, or other convenient means to avoid action. At work, for example, if there is some problem that needs resolution, we say, "I can't do anything about it; it's the company's or my boss' responsibility to fix it." In our local community we back away from challenges that face us saying, "I am only one voice; I have nothing positive to contribute." We vote with our feet and do little or nothing to assist. In our families we aim to keep peace and, at times, therefore, will not do what is necessary to correct problematic situations. We hide behind the facade of ignorance or inability in our failure to act. There are numerous problems within our contemporary Church. What are we doing to fix them? One might rightly say, "It's tough to fight City Hall," whether that be the government or the Church, but if we simply remain passive then nothing positive will ever happen. If such an attitude had prevailed in the early 1930s the Great Depression and its consequent human misery would have been much more prolonged.

Let us, therefore, not stand idly by, but rather do what is necessary to fix the problems we face as individuals, family, community, or Church. Let us as James says, act on the word and not merely listen. The road will not always be easy, but we can expect nothing less than the way our Master trod. Let us follow Jesus' lead, to death, but eventually to resurrection and eternal life.

Questions to Ponder:

1. Why do I too often hold back and refuse to get involved, especially when I know I can act?
2. What recent challenge has come my way that required my action? How did I meet the challenge?
3. Why do I often hide behind the letter of various laws and rules, doing the minimum, when I know I can do more?
4. Why do I cling to the attitude, "We have always done it this way!" when a new or more innovative method might work better?
5. How did I feel when I had the courage to boldly act to remedy a situation that needed the gifts I possessed?

God Overcomes All Obstacles

There once was a tree which live happily in a big forest with many other trees. Occasionally some of his brother and sister trees were cut down and the tree grieved, but when he discovered that his friends were reborn into some beautiful object that helped human beings, he no longer wept but actually looked forward to his turn to become something beautiful. Before long a wood carver came and examined the tree. The carver looked at the tree and imagined a beautiful figurine that could be made from its fine wood. The tree was delighted thinking that someday it would stand in a museum where people from all over the world could come and enjoy its beauty. The tree was so excited it jumped for joy, but just as it did the carver's initial blow came to the tree causing a huge gouge in the wood. The wood carver looked at the tree and thought that it could no longer serve his function, so he moved on to another tree.

Over the next few weeks and even months various other wood carvers came to the forest, looked at the tree but regretfully shook their heads saying, "It's is a pity. Such beautiful wood and exceptionally fine grain but now it is good for nothing but to be thrown into the fire." The poor tree wept. All around him he saw his fellow trees being made into beautiful objects, but he was good for nothing except to be chopped up and burned. He would die and never live forever as he had hoped.

Then one day a new carver appeared in the forest. He walked up to the tree sat down and looked at it with great concentration. After some time, he left and went away. Over the next several days the man returned each day looked at the tree but said nothing. Finally, one day the man did speak: "I see it now, the shape that you were meant to be." And then the man began to carve. He worked day and night with great passion to see the figure come before him. The tree did not understand what was happening. He had heard over and over again that he was ruined and could never be beautiful but as the new carver continued his work, he began to sense something remarkable was happening. He felt new life surge through his being and finally one day he emerged, a dancer, caught in precisely the proper moment that the contours of the damaged piece of wood dictated.

The man took his new masterpiece to a museum where all began to marvel at its beauty. Some said the flaw in the tree forced the artist to be more creative than usual if had worked with perfect materials. The tree really did not care. He knew he was reborn as a dancer and he danced away to the delight of all who passed that way.

This story is an excellent illustration of what is possible for those with sufficient patience and courage to wait and to work hard to overcome the difficulties and obstacles of life. Scripture helps us to better understand such challenges which come periodically in our lives. Like the tree we are called to have confidence that God's ability to aid us is ever present. Similarly, we are called to remove the barriers that keep us from others and from being the people God wants us to be.

Jeremiah proclaimed God's word to the Hebrews in the Southern Kingdom of Judah just prior to the infamous Babylonian Exile. The people of Judah were well aware of what happened to their northern neighbors, overrun by the Assyrians due to their lack of fidelity to God's word as proclaimed by people like Amos and Hosea. They or their ancestors had witnessed the demise of Israel and possibly feared a similar fate for themselves. But Jeremiah reminds the people that God will deliver them if they have patience and the courage to change: "See, I am going to bring them from the land of the north and gather them gather them from the farthest parts of the earth." (Jeremiah 31:8a) God, the prophet says, will console them and guide the community; God, in other words, will remove obstacles that keep the community from being the people God wants them to be.

Mark's Gospel (10:46-52) tells the wonderful story of Jesus' encounter with Bartimaeus, a blind man who stands alongside the road. Obviously, this man bore a major cross; he was given a major hurdle in his life. Yet, for reasons that are not explained by St. Mark, he had sufficient faith in Jesus to call out to him when he heard he was passing by. Jesus asks him what he wants, and he responds, "My teacher, let me see again." (10:51b)

Somehow, he knew that Jesus could remove the barrier and lighten his cross; his confidence in Christ was absolute.

The story of the tree and the two accounts from Scripture clearly show how God can remove the obstacles and barriers that keep us from being the people we want to be. Jesus completely understands our desires and our inability at times to be open to God's action. He can and will remove the obstacles and barriers from our lives, if we have enough patience to wait and courage to ask. A more significant problem, however, might be, not the obstacles placed before us over which we have no control, but rather those that we knowingly or unknowingly place between ourselves, others, and even God.

People often place barriers before them that will not allow them to be the people God calls them to be. We believe we are not intelligent enough, athletic enough, or possess enough talent to meet a goal or challenge. Thus, we shy away and make no effort, thinking any effort would be useless. Similarly, we place barriers in front of others, thinking that they are incapable or not sufficiently qualified to accomplish some task that is necessary. Our expectations are low, and because they are low, people are not allowed to attain their full capacity. These self-imposed barriers even happen in our relationship with God. Sometimes we say that God is not interested, God has too many other things to do, that my problems or my hurdles are so insignificant that even God cannot help me. However, the tree had sufficient patience, Bartimaeus had sufficient faith, and the Hebrews were sufficiently open to the prophet's words, allowing the various barriers that each found to be removed. So must it be with all of us.

Barriers come in two different forms--those from the outside over which we have no control and those which we ourselves create. Scripture clearly states that if we have sufficient patience and faith, God will overcome the various barriers and hurdles that beset us, the various crosses we are forced to bear. We must have sufficient faith to patiently wait for God to act, never losing hope, and ever confident. We must in a similar way remove the barriers that we impose against our own person, others, and God. We do have control over these and, therefore, it is up to us to act.

      The Eucharist, the high point of our Catholic Christian faith, strengthens us to be patient and have the courage to remove barriers in our lives. Therefore, as we gather around the sacred table of the Lord and are nourished by the real sacramental presence of Jesus, let us consider our need to be people of faith, people of patience. In other words, let us do our share to remove the barriers that keep us from accomplishing our goals; God will do the rest.

Questions to Ponder:

1. How do I at times place obstacles in my path that hinder me from doing what God asks?
2. When was the last time I gave up on some project or activity because I felt inadequate for the job?
3. What obstacles or roadblocks have I consciously or unconsciously placed before others, not allowing them to fully blossom?
4. How do I weather the storms that life throws my way? What defense mechanism have I created?
5. When I have been thrown off the normal path of life, how have I reacted?

Faith Conquers Fear

  Have you ever been truly afraid, so full of fear that you did not know what to do? I found myself in such a predicament on December 13, 1979. It was the day I met fear head on! At that time, I was assigned to a US Navy submarine. On the day in question I was "on watch" as the officer in charge of the nuclear reactor, the Engineering Officer of the Watch. My watch section was in the process of running engineering casualty drills, a normal, even routine function, which was conducted three or four times per week. One drill required that power be secured to the main engines, the primary means of propulsion. As the drill progressed the words which drive fear into anyone who has ever served on submarines were heard over the boat's announcement system, "Flooding, flooding in the operations compartment."
  The words struck me powerfully and fear was at the doorstep. The men with whom I was working were also struck with fear. We needed to act swiftly to keep the boat from sinking. We had run many drills, but this was different. This was an actual casualty; the boat was in serious jeopardy. The only way to overcome fear was to meet it head on. We had to respond as we had been trained. We had to find faith in our ability to think and act, and confidence in the machinery which we operated. The Engineer, my superior officer, left the engineering spaces and gave me the order, "Get the main engines on the line." We did just that - in less than five minutes the boat was on the surface. The crew was quite shaken, but we were safe. Fear had been conquered; faith had won the day!
  Scripture speaks about how faith can overcome fear, if we will only allow it to happen. Mark's Gospel provides an excellent example in the famous story of Jesus calming the storm on the lake. Jesus and his close friends are on the lake, the Sea of Galilee. It is not a large body of water, but storms do arise. The combination of the weather and nightfall produced fear in the minds of the apostles. Jesus seems oblivious to the whole matter. Mark tells us that he was asleep on a cushion. Jesus has absolute

confidence and trust; the disciples, on the other hand, have little of both. The storm comes and the apostles are terrified. They implore Jesus to do something. "Teacher, do you care that we are perishing?' (Mark 4:38b) Jesus, in a rather disgruntled tone responds, "Why are you afraid? Have you still no faith?" (Mark 4:40) Jesus calms the storm. The rain ceases and the wind dies down. The apostles are overcome by awe.

In this passage Jesus demonstrates his ability to triumph over the elements of nature. But who can do what Jesus does? As the apostles state, "Who is this, that even the wind and the sea obey him?" (Mark 4:41b) The Book of Job provides an answer to the apostles' question. Responding to Job's query, the Lord says, "Or who shut in the sea with doors when it burst out from the womb—when I made the clouds its garment and thick darkness its swaddling band." (Job 38:8-9) By understanding Job, we should see that, not only has Jesus calmed the storm and demonstrated the triumph of faith over fear; he has proven that he is God as well. That is precisely why Mark says the apostles were in awe at Jesus. From this day forward, he could only be seen as God, never again as a mere man.

We might ask ourselves, what is the opposite of fear? Most people probably would answer that courage or bravery is the opposite of fear. But Scripture tells us that the opposite of fear is faith. Faith conquers the fears of our lives, our community and our world. Fear, unfortunately, is rampant in our world. Economic strife in countries, local communities, and even families threatens the stability of society and instills fear. The North-South split in the hemispheres of the world, where the North are the haves and the South the have-nots, also raises the specter of fear. There is an ever-present fear of war and hostility in the many hotbeds of our world, such as the Middle East. There is the constant threat of international terrorism; we are often paralyzed by fear.

How do we overcome the fear that surrounds us? We can build more arms and make ourselves feel secure. We can restrict access at airports to keep evil elements away. We can encourage nations and governments to enact laws which serve the common good, not just a few. All of these ideas serve a purpose and may be helpful in eliminating fear. But what about Jesus' answer to fear?

How does he suggest we calm the storms of our lives? St. Paul provides an answer. Writing to the Corinthians (II Corinthians 5:14-17) he says that we should live for others as Christ lived for us. This is a way to cast out personal fear and center on the needs of others. Such action demonstrates the faith which Jesus showed the night he calmed the storm on the lake. Faith is the ultimate answer to fear. We need to advance our faith and our ability to act. We must increase our faith in those people around us and their ability to help. In the end our faith in God must be our refuge and strength. Let us demonstrate faith and use it to conquer the fears of our world and our own person. Let the permanent solution to fear be found in Christ, our brother, Savior, and Lord!

Questions to Ponder:

1. We have all been challenged by the element of fear in our lives. What has been my response?
2. Have I run away in fear from my challenges; have I avoided the situation, or, have I met fear head on and challenged it with faith?
3. When was the last time I felt "paralyzed" by a situation, not knowing where to go or how to act?
4. What can I do to alleviate and conquer the fears that plague my life?
5. Why do I place my hopes in the things of the world when I know that the only ultimate cure to any and all fears is my faith in the Lord?

Trials of Faith

On Boxer Day, December 26, 2004, a massive earthquake, registering 9.2 on the Richter scale, the third greatest recorded earthquake in history, struck off the west coast of Sumatra. The earthquake itself did considerable damage to that Indonesian island, but the tsunami that it generated, spreading in all directions, killed 230,000 people in 11 countries throughout the regions of Southeast Asia, the Indian sub-continent, and Indonesia. Yet, one family miraculously survived this ordeal intact, even though they were literally in the eye of the storm.

The Alvarez family from Spain, Quique the father, Maria his wife, and their three children Lucas, Tomas, and Simon, were guests at the Orchid Resort in Thailand when the tsunami struck. Maria, a physician, and her eldest son Lucas were swept away by the raging waters. Underwater approximately three minutes, Maria still managed to rise to the surface. Struck by much of the debris that the giant wave had swept away, her left leg was severely injured. She managed to find Lucas who was clinging to a tree that managed to survive the water's force. Lucas assisted his mother to climb to relative safety in the branches of the tree. Meanwhile, Quique, the father of the family, and his two younger sons, who were also swept away, wound up somewhat miraculously together on the upper floor of a resort hotel which was not completely destroyed. Although battered and bruised these three, along with the eldest son Lucas, were not injured severely by the tsunami.

Not knowing the status of his wife and oldest son, Quique began to search. The devastation from the tsunami was so massive that refugee camps and makeshift field hospitals were set up in any accessible area. Again, somewhat miraculously, some local villagers found Maria and Lucas and brought them to one of these hospitals. Her chances of survival were not great, but she and her son had faith. Similarly, her husband, expressing his great faith, was convinced that his wife and son were alive and that, with perseverance, he could find them. It took several days, during which Maria was fortunate enough to receive proper care, saving not only her life, but her leg as well. Finally reunited, the family was grateful that through perseverance and faith they had found each other.

The story of the miraculous survival of the Alvarez family is a good example of how perseverance and faith can lead us to conquer even the most severe trials of life. Scripture teaches us a similar message. The task of being a prophet in ancient Israel was anything but easy. Some of the prophets did not want the job. Jonah ran away from God's call until he was captured by the whale; Amos and others told God they were not qualified. All of the prophets proclaimed God's message, but most of the time their words fell on deaf ears or were rejected outright. People did not want to change or reform their lives. Some of the prophets, like Jeremiah, were threatened with bodily harm. Jeremiah was cast into a cistern and left to die. The plot had been approved by Zedekiah, the king, one who certainly should have known better. Jeremiah was tested; his experience was a great trial. He was able, however, to see beyond the immediate, to grow from the experience, and with a clear belief keep his eyes fixed on what God asked of him.

Luke the evangelist relates words that on our first hearing do not sound like they would come from the mouth of Jesus. We read, "I came to bring fire to the earth, and how I wish it were already kindled! ... Do you think that I have come to bring peace to the earth? No, I tell you. But rather division." (Luke 12:49, 51) He goes on to say that he will divide families, father against son, mother against daughter. What the Lord in essence is saying is that trials and tests will come our way and we must be ready to work through them to get to the other side. We all know that there are many trials in life. All of us experience trials in our daily work. It is a trial to hold our temper when a co-worker is lazy, unreliable, or irritable, when one's inability to perform causes more work for us. It is a trial when the boss comes to us with a task that must be completed yesterday, knowing that on our desk there are already ten items with due dates that have passed. There are many trials in our personal life. Injury, sickness or death to a family member or close friend is a trial which calls upon our courage, interior strength, and faith. Some people face the trial of exercising "tough love" toward another. Addictions to alcohol, drugs, or even sex create a trial where one must say that because I love you, I will not aid your habit. There are certainly trials in the Church. Contemporary issues raise significant questions that force us to harmonize our beliefs with those of the Church and to discover our place and vocation within the Christian call to holiness.

The many trials of life require that we look beyond the immediate to discover the goal we seek. The author of the Letter to the Hebrews tells us there is a reason that we must persevere in running the race. We are to keep our eyes fixed on Jesus, "the pioneer and perfecter of our faith." (Hebrews 12:2) The Lord was forced to endure many trials. He was opposed by people on all sides, His message was rejected by many, and he was betrayed and abandoned by those he knew best. Through it all, however, Jesus was able to persevere because he knew that he would one day return to God. Such must be our hope and prayer as well.

The story of the Alvarez family from Spain, depicted in the motion picture "The Impossible," while miraculous, does nonetheless, demonstrate that with God all things are possible. Similarly, scripture tells us that if we can persevere through the trials and tribulations of life, we will gain an even greater prize. The goal we seek is worth every ounce of effort we can give. St. Paul (I Corinthians 2:9) has beautifully described what we believe, "What no eye has seen, nor ear heard, not the human heart conceived, what God has prepared for those who love him." Let us keep our eyes on Jesus and endure the trials of life. Our reward will be eternal life.

Questions to Ponder:

1. When tragedy strikes and there seems to be no hope, what has been my reaction?
2. What have I done to help others safely negotiate the trials that have come my way?
3. When I am burdened with many responsibilities, how do I set my priorities in accomplishing tasks?
4. What lessons in life have I learned when trials come my way?
5. What can I learn from the life of Jesus, one filled with trials, that can assist me in negotiating the obstacles in my life?

Encountering Christ, the Merciful One

The Atlantic slave trade was, unquestionably, one of the darkest moments in human history of the Common Era. Between 1450 and 1850 twelve million sub-Saharan Africans were ferried from their homeland, most arriving in the New World. Whether these men and women were sold to traders, kidnaped, or obtained as a booty of war, they were all moved against their will and placed in roles of total servitude. African slaves, from the time of their purchase in Africa to their sale in the Americas, were treated in the most inhumane ways, but it was the voyage to the New World, known by historians as the Middle Passage, that was most gruesome. Slaves were herded aboard vessels and shackled in their places below decks. The average male was given a mere seven square feet of space. The air was foul and made one nauseous, food and water were minimal, and disease was rampant. Often as many as 25% of the Africans died before they reached their destinations. When they arrived their condition was, as one can only imagine, poor. The wretched conditions and inhuman treatment were characteristic of the mentality concerning slaves; they were property, not human beings.

Cartagena, located along the northern coast of what is today Colombia, was a major port of debarkation for slave vessels. While the Church had been established for more than fifty years in the area, few people had ever questioned slavery let alone reached out to those who, through no intention of their own, were forced to participate. In 1610, however, a Spanish Jesuit named Peter Claver, arrived in Cartagena and quickly took up a personal ministry to the approximately 10,000 Black Africans who arrived annually. When a slave ship arrived the men, women, and children onboard were herded together in pens without any medical attention or other assistance. Peter Claver, imitating the work of his mentor, Fr. Alfonso de Sandoval, took the time necessary to visit the slaves, attending to their physical needs with food and medicine. When the slaves were sent to the mines, as was generally the case on the west coast of South America, Claver would go and nurse them, generally without the permission of owners, placing himself in jeopardy. He was not concerned about what others would think of him; all that mattered was that his service was needed. Peter Claver called himself, "the slave of the slaves forever." Many had the opportunity to help but they seemed to ignore the situation or lacked the courage to act. Others may have noticed but did not have the courage to act.

Peter Claver's ministry to African slaves did not preclude him from caring for others, including condemned criminals whom he prepared for death, visiting local hospitals, and conducting an annual mission to traders and seamen in the region. Through his efforts many Africans slaves and others found the faith.

Peter Claver died in 1654 and was recognized with a huge funeral arranged by the slaves and others he assisted. He was canonized in 1888 and declared at the time the patron of all missionary enterprises among Black Africans. He was a man who when given the opportunity to encounter one less fortunate than himself, and in response to his faith, did precisely what Jesus commands in the Scriptures, to show compassion and care for others. We are challenged to do the same.

Certainly, one of the most well-known passages in the whole New Testament is the Parable of the Good Samaritan, found in Luke 10: 25-37. The passage forces us to ask a question: If we were given a special chance to be a neighbor and show mercy, how would we respond? This parable could be given another name, "The man who manifested faith through mercy." The story presents a traveler who has encountered robbers, something we unfortunately hear about all too often in our own day. The man is injured; he is unable to care for himself. We are told that three passersby are given the opportunity to help, to befriend the injured man, to encounter God by showing mercy. The first two, the priest and the Levite, were highly respected members of the community, the kind of people society appreciates and in whom trust is placed. These two, one-by-one, come upon the scene. They have the opportunity to help, but they do not take advantage of the opportunity afforded them. As St. Luke says, they simply passed by. These men decided to follow the Mosaic Law which required ritual purity, rather than risk becoming unclean through contact with the injured man. The third man who comes upon the scene is a Samaritan. He was from the northern part of Israel. Samaria was the ancient land of the ten lost tribes conquered some 700 years before Jesus' birth. Jews did not trust Samaritans; they would never be accepted in Hebrew society. They were not considered worthy of respect. Yet, this third man, the one hated by everyone and was given no respect or chance in life, was the one who took the opportunity God gave him, to be neighbor to another.

God gives us many chances, many opportunities, but do we use the opportunity, take advantage of the possibility, or do we merely pass by? The opportunity to be a neighbor, to show that we care and, in the process, show the face of God to others happens each day. Almost daily we encounter people who are hurt. It may be a person who hurts physically, like the man who fell among robbers. More often, however, we will find people who hurt inside, someone who has been wounded by the words and actions of others, by events, by the cruelty of the world.

When someone hurts, when someone wants to talk, do we do as the priest and Levite and pass by or do we take the time and make the effort of the Samaritan and show God to others? We cannot always be there for others - there would be nothing left for ourselves. But what is our attitude? Is our heart open like the Samaritan or closed like the priest and Levite? Each one of us must answer this most challenging question!

The tendency to "pass by" the situation before us can happen to all, regardless of our status in life. Children by ignoring their friends or refusing friendship say I don't need you; you are not my neighbor. Adults who continually refuse to respond to God's call found in the faces and voices of neighbors, the sick, the poor, the stranger say, I don't need you; you are not my neighbor. When we always care more for ourselves and seemingly forget the needs of others, we say is essence, you are not important; I will pass you by. In such cases what opportunities we miss. God is so near; we only need to open our eyes and see him!

Answering the call of the Lord to be neighbor is not too difficult when we like an individual or believe that our actions will one day result in some reciprocity. On the other hand, when we sense that nothing will come our way in return, we, at times, hesitate. Peter Claver ran afoul of civic and religious leaders and endured conditions that others would not even consider in carrying out Jesus' edict to be neighbor and not pass by. He knew he would get nothing in return, but that did not change his response. Are we ready for the challenge? Can we stop long enough to be a true neighbor to a person in need, physically, emotionally or spiritually? Can we respond to the Lord's exhortation on mercy, "Go and do likewise?" All of us must answer!

Questions to Ponder:

1. In today's world, "Who is my neighbor?" How would I answer?
2. When was the last time I chose compassion over adherence to some law or regulation which suggested I act in a way contrary to my Christian faith?
3. How have I manifested the compassion of Jesus when dealing with colleagues at work and those whom I encounter on a regular basis?
4. How have I treated the contemporary "Samaritans" in society, those who have been rejected by all and stand on the margins?
5. What opportunities have come my way to assist those in need and I chose to simply pass by, missing an opportunity to encounter God?

Faith, Discipleship and Ministry

Finding the Lost

Baseball fans today might not recall the name Branch Rickey, but for what he did for America's national pastime he should not only be known but enshrined in a place of honor. Rickey was raised in Ohio in a family with a strict Protestant moral ethic. He understood the value of people and the equality each person had in the eyes of God. This fundamental belief and his consequent pioneering efforts on the behalf of the "lost" would bring him to baseball's coveted Hall of Fame.

Branch Rickey played baseball in college and was good enough to play a few years professionally, but his great claim to fame came not on the field but in the front office of major league baseball. After his brief stint on the field, he managed the St. Louis Cardinals for a few years in the 1920s, but then he moved into the front office as President and General Manager of the team. His wise decision-making transformed St. Louis from a team that was second rate to a World Series champion. In fact, St. Louis won the series three times during his over twenty years with the team, as manager or executive.

In 1942, however, Rickey moved east to Brooklyn to take up the General Manager position with the Dodgers. Always looking for good talent and ever cognizant of his strong belief in equality of all human beings, Rickey heard about a fabulous athlete who had attended UCLA. His name was Jackie Robinson. Robinson was an athlete who could do it all, but his great forte was track and field. Nonetheless, Rickey spoke to Robinson and asked him if he was interested in playing major league baseball. There was only one major problem--Robinson was African American and there had never been a Black player in the major leagues. Robinson agreed to Rickey's terms. Basically, Rickey asked the young athlete to ignore the slurs, inappropriate actions, and general rejection that was certain to come when he, an African American, would step on the diamond of a major league team. When Jackie Robinson joined the Dodgers in 1947 all that Rickey anticipated came true, but Robinson was up to the test. He proved his mettle beyond expectation, playing for 10 years with distinction. He was voted rookie of the year in 1947 and most valuable player in 1949; he was six times selected to the National League All-Star team.

In 1955, Branch Rickey moved again, this time to Pittsburgh to another front office job. While the Pirates as a team did not markedly improve under his direction, he again took the bold step of reaching out to another "lost" group who had previously been ignored by major league baseball. In 1955 he recruited and signed Roberto Clemente, who became the first Hispanic player in the major leagues. Like Robinson 10 years earlier, Clemente was a star and paved the way for so many others to follow, some whose names are more contemporary heroes: Alex Rodriguez and David Ortiz.

Branch Rickey took a chance, went out on a limb, to bring to prominence people who had been placed on the margins simply because of the color of their skin or their ethnic background. Jesus was color blind when it came to people; all were acceptable and had merit. Scripture provides many examples of this reality. Jesus' example of reaching out to all, seeking the lost and forsaken, must be an example for all of us to follow.

St. Luke (19:1-10) tells the story of Zacchaeus, one who from the Jewish perspective was "lost." A tax collector, like Matthew, he would have been placed on the margins by Hebrew society, but Jesus notices him as he entered Jericho and in a public way brings him into his fold. Certainly, those observing the scene must have been shocked that Jesus invited himself to the home of the tax collector for a meal. Why would this man, who claimed to be so close to God and did such miraculous works, intentionally associate with someone who was hated, a nobody in Jewish society, a person who had lost his way? Clearly, Jesus is trying to teach a lesson that God's message goes out to all people; no one is excluded. Jesus is preaching a message of inclusivity; he is reversing the conventional wisdom of the day. As Jesus says, "For the Son of Man came to seek out and to save the lost." (Luke 19:10)

However, Jesus' action should not have been that unexpected. The wisdom literature of the Hebrew Scriptures clearly says that God's mercy, compassion, and concern is universal. We read, "But you are merciful to all, for you can do all things, and you overlook people's sins, so that they may repent." (Wisdom 11:23) God rejects no one, for he is the creator of all. Since God wills that things exist, it is impossible that he would do anything other than preserve what he created. These words, applied to Zacchaeus, suggest the reason Jesus overtly sought him out and made him an example for all who observed these events. The message was clear, God looks for and rescues the lost.

Jesus' outreach to Zacchaeus, a manifestation of God's preservation of life, impacts us in two significant ways. First, the Lord's action gives us reason for hope in our lives. There are times when we are lost, when our natural and proper direction toward God is thrown out of whack and we move in ways which may even be directly opposed to God. Since we are the creation of God, we can take solace in the fact that the Lord will never abandon us, but rather, using the image of Francis Thompson's epic poem, "The Hound of Heaven," we know that God leaves no stone unturned in a diligent search for us. This should be a great consolation when we realize we have gone astray. But Jesus' action with a tax collector also challenges us to act in a similar way. Too often we reject individuals or groups for many varied, but seldom proper, reasons. Many members of society today are lost, stand on the margins, and are not allowed to participate fully. In the time of Branch Rickey, as hard as it might be to conceive today, Black and Hispanic athletes were not allowed to participate in professional sports. They were lost, but through persistence, they were found through the efforts of one courageous man. We must be like Rickey and seek out the lost of our society and bring them to the fold as did Jesus in his outreach to Zacchaeus. As one community of faith, old and young, male and female, Black, White, Asian, Hispanic, native or immigrant, let us be aware that God will find us and we must have the courage to seek and to find others, to the glory and praise of God.

Questions to Ponder:

1. How have I reached out recently to those who stand on the margins of society?
2. When I have been ignored, treated unfairly or held in contempt by others, how have I reacted?
3. What has been my attitude toward immigrants and others who stand on the margins of contemporary society?
4. Why have I at times rejected the Lord's call in my life?
5. What do I need to do to see beyond the everyday activities of life so as to believe that God is always acting for our betterment and benefit?

Part II: Essays on Discipleship

Overview

The road to Jesus and life eternal must begin with being people of faith, but unless that faith leads to action, we will never find our way home to God. St. James (2:14-17) very powerfully reminds us:

> What good is it, my brothers and sisters, if you say you have faith but do not have works? Can faith save you? If a brother or sister is naked and lacks daily food, and one of you says to them, "Go in peace; keep warm and eat your fill," and yet do not supply their bodily needs, what is the good of that? So faith by itself, if it has no works, is dead.

As followers of Jesus, faith is the seed from which the good works that we do, the process of discipleship, must flow. As described in Part I, the necessity of faith is absolute, but, as James suggests, if we do not utilize that faith in a positive way to assist others, then our religious convictions and hopes are empty or even possibly misguided.

Before we can get to the point of conducting ministry, we must understand our need to be disciples of Jesus Christ. Presumably Peter and the other 11 original apostles whom Jesus called to be his inner circle possessed faith. For the people and the time, it would have been a strong Jewish faith centered in monotheism, a radical idea for the polytheistic Greco-Roman world, and the Law, not only the Decalogue, but all 613 prescriptions and proscriptions articulated in the Pentateuch. But when Jesus called the apostles, their life of faith moved in a different direction; they became the first disciples, namely followers, of Christ. Over time that original group of 12 expanded, including the 72 disciples mentioned in the Gospel of Luke (10:1-7), many unmentioned people, as well as many faithful women who, we must recall, with the first witnesses of the resurrection.

Discipleship requires one to take the basic faith given us by God, the faith that we must continually nurture and strengthen, and internalize it. This will lead to an absolute and unbending willingness to follow Jesus, wherever that may take us and whatever he may ask us to do. It is faith that gives us the strength to place our lives into the hands of God. Since by nature humans seek to control as much as they can, but especially their own lives, discipleship requires great interior strength, because the places we go and the times we are sent might not always be convenient or desirable. Yet, that is precisely what discipleship requires. Let us hope that we, like the apostles can, not only hear the call to discipleship, but unselfishly and rapidly respond and follow in the footsteps of Jesus.

The Challenge of Tough Love

The time was November 1930. The place was the Memorial Coliseum in Los Angeles, California. The event was the annual gridiron clash between college football powerhouses, Notre Dame and the University of Southern California. On one side of the field decorated in cardinal and gold stood Howard Jones, the successful and well-respected football coach at USC. On the visitor's side of the field stood Knute Rockne, arguably the most famous college football coach of all time. The experts, the odds makers, had predicted that the game would not be close; they favored USC by 15 points.

That year Notre Dame used its famous "box" formation as a version of the old single wing offense. Frank Corridio, the Irish quarterback, had been a star that season and had earned the honored distinction of "All American." Corridio, however, would not be a major factor in the game. The stars would be two rather unheralded players, Bucky O'Connor, a third-team halfback, who played only because of injuries to teammates, and Hal "Watch-dial" Metzger, a relatively small running guard.

The opening play from scrimmage was a foreshadowing of the afternoon's events. O'Connor took a handoff and behind the blocking of Metzger, who hit one man, pick himself up and hit a second and then a third, ran 80 yards for a touchdown. Notre Dame never looked back. When the dust had cleared, the spikes had been hung up, and all the fans had gone home, the scoreboard read, Notre Dame - 27, USC - 0. The Irish had scored a great victory, an upset. Yet, Notre Dame lost something much greater that day; Knute Rockne had coached his last game. He would die the next spring on March 31 in an infamous plane crash.

Knute Rockne was a coach; he was a friend. Above all he was a man who loved. Rockne was successful, the most successful football coach in Notre Dame history. Why was he successful? Certainly, he had great players. Rockne coached some of the best players of the day, many of whom, like Frank Corridio, and the fabled "Four Horsemen" who earned the coveted title of "All

American." Rockne was successful, however, because he was a man who had learned to love and thereby to teach responsibility.

Playing ball for Knute Rockne was not easy; he was tough on his players. A second-rate performance or effort was not satisfactory. If a player did not give his all, he didn't play long for Rock. If there was something wrong, he would point out the error. His direction, his method of coaching, was in a very real way a form of love, a love which taught responsibility to his players.

Scripture speaks of our need to be responsible to others as the one debt of love which we owe to all. The prophet Ezekiel (33:7) tells us that we must take our responsibility seriously to challenge others. We read: "So you, mortal, I have made a sentinel for the house of Israel; whenever you hear a word from my mouth, you shall give them warning from me." He goes on to say that if we see an individual in error, then we must take the time to correct that person. Equally we could say that if we see someone in need in a more general sense, then we need to aid that person. If we refuse to aid another, if we will not take the time to correct someone who is in error, then we will be held accountable for our failure to act.

In Matthew's Gospel Jesus also says that we must take responsibility for others. When speaking to the apostles, Jesus said: "If another member of the church sins against you, go and point out the fault when the two of you are alone. If the member listens to you, you have regained that one." (Matthew 18:15) Today we call Jesus' challenge fraternal correction. Jesus does tell us that we need to use proper methods when we correct a person, but in the end, we must not fail to act. We must do what is necessary. The Lord also says that we must be decisive in what we do. As he says, "Whatever you bind on earth, will be bound in heaven and whatever you loose on earth will be loosed in heaven." (Matthew 18:19)

Fraternal correction, challenging others, when done properly and with the correct attitude, truly is an act of love. It is not an act of love that is easily visible, but it is one that is absolutely essential. St. Paul referred to this same love when writing to the Christian community at Rome: "Owe no one anything, except to love one another, for the one who loves another has fulfilled the law." (Romans 13: 8) Paul is claiming, in other words, if we have loved we have paid our debt; we need do nothing more.

Learning to love is a great challenge. Some forms of love, such as the Greek concept of *eros* or romantic love, come quite naturally. Certainly, romantic love takes work; it is not easy. But *eros* is generated by feelings of the heart; it does not come from the brain. Love can and must be deeper and broader than our feelings alone. Love means being honest; it is tough love. That might mean for each of us that we need to separate ourselves from an individual, an idea or a movement which gets us nowhere, at least nowhere we need or want to be. Tough love also could mean having the courage to challenge someone we love very much and tell that person there is a problem that needs to be corrected. It could mean refusing to aid the addiction of someone we love. It might mean refusing to participate in unethical work practices and challenging others to follow your lead.

Love means being responsible; love is a challenge. It is not easy to challenge others, to be confrontational especially in a society which tells us to mind our own business and not get involved. Yet, the Bible clearly tells us that we must be responsible to others, as the only debt of love that we owe. Let us realize that love is much more than flowers sent, kinds words spoken, and signs of affection. Knute Rockne showed tough love as a coach and through that action taught responsibility. In the process he earned a permanent place in the annals of sports history. Let us also know that we too must show love and demonstrate it by being responsible, so that we also can earn a permanent place, in eternal life with God.

Questions to Ponder:

1. When the situation required it, in my family, at work, or in the community where I live, how did I exercise "tough love?"
2. What debts of love do I owe to others? What plan do I have to fulfill my obligations to others?
3. For me, what does responsibility entail in the various aspects of my life?
4. What lessons have I learned when tough love was used in my life? How can I use that experience positively for others?
5. What has been my response when others fail to meet their responsibilities, including their responsibilities to me?

Demonstrating God's Love to Others

On the battlefield a chaplain encountered a soldier lying wounded and in pain in a foxhole. "Would you like me to read you a passage from the Bible," asked the chaplain. The young soldier could only respond, "I'm so thirsty." Without another word the chaplain ran off, found a canteen, poured the man a cup of water, and helped him drink. The soldier squirmed about— "I'm very uncomfortable," he groaned. Again, the chaplain without a second thought stripped off his overcoat, rolled it in a ball and placed it under the young man's head as a pillow. The soldier began to shiver— "I'm so cold," he whispered. The chaplain took off his own jacket and sweater and placed them over the injured man. Then the soldier looked the chaplain straight in the eye and said, "Now if there is anything in that book which will allow another person to do more than you have already done for me, then please read it because I would like to hear it."

Three young people were discussing new translations of the Bible. One person said, "I like the New American Bible. It is clearer than older translations and is easier to read." Another person said, "I like the Jerusalem Bible. It too is clear, but it is more poetic, and I can use it in prayer." A third person spoke, "I like my mother's version best. She translated the Bible into action so that I can apply it to my daily life."

An international group of young adults met for one week to discuss various techniques of evangelization. During their lively discussions and sessions, they saw many movies and videos, heard several presentations, listened to tapes, and were introduced to many books and scholarly essays. When the week had concluded and the all the participants gathered together for a wrap-up session, one young woman from Africa rose and gave her opinion. "In my country when we hear that a pagan village is ready for Christianity, we do not send movies, books or even missionaries. We send the best Christian family we can find for the example of a good family is a more powerful proclamation of the Gospel than all the books in the world."

Three short but different stories, but one common theme--what we do is very important. We are all called to be evangelists through the words of our mouth and the actions we daily perform. Scripture challenges us in a similar way.

Isaiah, in the second third (chapters 40-55) of his long book of prophecy, writes to the Hebrew people after their return from exile in Babylon. They were there because in the past the community has not treated each other with love. The rich and powerful oppressed the weak and the poor. Now, however, Isaiah says it is a new day for Israel. If the people can change, if they will share their food, shelter the oppressed and the homeless, and clothe the naked, then the light will come to them. Their wound will be healed. When the people call upon God, God will answer. God will be present when the people cry for help. If the people remove those obstacles which drove them into exile--oppression, malicious speech, and false accusations--then the light will come. (Isaiah 58:7-10) In other words, if the people demonstrate God's love to each other, the Lord will answer their prayers and fulfill their needs.

In Matthew's Gospel Jesus speaks of being salt and light. He says, "You are the salt of the earth; … You are the light of the world." (5:13a, 14a) We know that salt enhances food; it makes it taste better. However, if the people lose their drive, their zeal for God, then like salt which goes flat and is tasteless, so will the people be useless and will trampled underfoot. The people are to shine brightly, not as a lamp under a bushel basket but as one on a stand where all can see. Others must see the goodness in their acts and how they give glory to God.

We must demonstrate God's love to others; we must set the example. We are to do our best to salt the earth and become the light of the world. What we do is very important. Our actions tell others who we are and what we believe. Do our actions tell other people that we belong to Christ, that our total allegiance is with God? Do others see in us the picture we want to portray?

We must bring Christ to all that we do and to all whom we encounter. If you are in school, then bring Christ to the classroom. Refuse to compromise your values to those of the world. Offer a better alternative to the contemporary vices of laziness, gangs, drugs, alcohol, and sex. If you work in business, then bring Christ to the office. Take an ethical approach to your work and refuse to take shortcuts which may ill-affect others. Do your work in a righteous manner; your integrity is important. Make certain that peers, superiors, and subordinates alike know that you stand with God. If you work at home or are retired, then bring Christ to those whom you encounter each day. Make certain that those at the market, in the bank or at the day care or senior centers know that Jesus is important in your life.

What we do is very important. The chaplain's unselfish actions spoke more clearly to the soldier than any passage from the Bible could have done. A good Christian family demonstrates the Gospel message more powerfully than a whole host of books. When translated into action, the Bible can be best applied to our daily lives. Let us, therefore, demonstrate God's love to others; let us set the best example we can. May the light of Christ shine through us to brighten our world today and each day of our lives!

Questions to Ponder:

1. How have I recently manifested the slogan, "Actions speak louder than words?"
2. How have I seen Jesus manifested through the actions of others?
3. What have I done recently to bring the face of Christ to others?
4. What does it mean to me to serve others and by our actions serve Jesus himself?
5. What more must I do to truly say I am model, faithful and responsible Christian?

Modeling the Faithfulness of God

John Gray wore the badge of Constable, Number 90 for the police force of Edinburgh, Scotland. The time was the mid-19th century. As a Constable John was required to have a watchdog and thus was given one for this purpose, but it is not clear what type of dog he was originally given. It seems, however, that the two did not get along and thus, obliged to keep the regulations, John was required to find another watchdog. He chose a Skye Terrier that was about six months old. He named the dog Bobby, an appropriate name for a watchdog for a police officer in Great Britain. Bobby now became a part of John Gray's life. His shaggy hair from his long body hung over his eyes; his stump of a tale wagged continually. He was tenacious in character, distrustful of strangers, but devoted to John and his friends and friends. He was courageous, but not aggressive. No other sort of dog has the tenacity, cockiness, and sparkle possessed by a Skye Terrier.

In his duties as a Constable, Gray met many friends and had to deal with many difficult situations. Bobby was always close to his master's heels. Often John Gray and his faithful dog Bobby would take a leisurely walk to Greyfriar's Place, a coffee shop owned by William Ramsay. They had a favorite seat and watched the patrons come in and go out of the establishment. One of Gray's duties was to keep watch on cattle pens at night to make sure there was no theft. Again, Bobby was always close beside.

In October 1857, the nights were cold and damp, yet John Gray and Bobby took their watch as usual. John developed a severe cold. Eventually he was treated by a local doctor who realized that he was in the first stages of tuberculosis. Eventually John became weaker and weaker until on February 8, 1858 he died with Bobby laying at his feet. For the next 14 years until his own death in 1872, the faithful Skye Terrier, Bobby, stood vigil at his master's grave. Even though regulations did not allow animals in the cemetery, Bobby's case was different. Each morning Bobby would be found lying on his master's grave. Local people, having pity on the dog, brought him food and water, but he remained faithful to his master's memory all of those years. He never wavered.

Greyfriar's Bobby has been immortalized with a statute that even today stands prominently in a main square of Edinburgh. This faithful dog, like similar stories, for example the story of Hachi, a faithful Akita who waited daily for nine years at a train station for his master to return, provide powerful examples of an important message found in Scripture, our need to model the faithfulness of God

Salvation history is the story of God's fidelity to the Hebrew people, which found its apex and finest hour in the life and ministry of Jesus Christ. God faithfully led the Hebrews out of slavery in Egypt, planted them in the Promised Land, and provided for their every need. Yet, the people were often unfaithful, leading to the destruction of the Northern Kingdom of Israel and exile for the Southern Kingdom of Judah. Nevertheless, the prophet Isaiah tells us that God is ever faithful, without regard to our failures. He tells the Hebrews in exile using a powerful metaphor: "Can a woman forget her nursing child, or show no compassion for the child of her womb? Even these may forget, yet I will not forget you." (Isaiah 49:15) Certainly this is a powerful image to which any human can relate. The faithfulness of God is constant and overflowing. Similarly, in his Sermon on the Mount (6:24-34), Jesus provides additional evidence to the faithfulness of God. God takes care of the birds of the sky; will God not be even more faithful in taking care of his greatest creation, humanity? Jesus tells his disciples that they should stop worrying and express greater faith. God will take care of them if they will only trust him.

Faithfulness, as found in famous stories, such as Greyfriar's Bobby or Hachi, is a quality that we need very badly in our world. We need to be people who are faithful in every aspect of life. We must be faithful in our relationships with one another, whether that be marriage, friendships, associations at work, or relations with neighbors down the street. It is very easy to fall away from being faithful to our relationships, whatever they might be, and thus the challenge presented in Scripture is significant. We must be faithful to our responsibilities, at home, at work, in our town or city, and with our church. We cannot walk away, shirk or be lazy when it comes to our responsibilities. People, time, and opportunities have been given to us by God to be utilized properly. If we fail to be faithful to our responsibilities and to others, we are in essence being irresponsible and faithless to God. Our formal faith as exercised through prayer, celebration of the sacraments, and participation in the community of faith, that is the Church, expresses our faithfulness to God, but we do so also through our fidelity to one another and our responsibilities.

Greyfriar's Bobby was a faithful Skye Terrier, who has been immortalized in bronze, story, and legend. The faithfulness he demonstrated to his master can be an example of how we must always seek to be faithful to our ultimate master, Jesus. Let us consider how faithful we have been to our commitments, seeking to model our lives after Jesus, the one who was ever faithful, the one who died to set us free, the one who will always be our brother, Savior, and Lord.

Questions to Ponder:

1. What does fidelity to God mean to me? How has it been manifested in my life?
2. How faithful have I been to the various responsibilities—people, work, and God—in my life?
3. How have I reacted when people have not met their responsibilities toward me or to groups or institutions to which I belong?
4. Why do I at times ignore the needs of others, especially the most vulnerable in our society?
5. What more must I do to truly say I can be a model for what it means to a faithful and responsible Christian?

Feeding Each Other

There is an ancient Asian tale which describes the difference between heaven and hell. The image of hell begins with the description of a long banquet-like table around which many are seated preparing to eat. The meal is ready, abundant, and on the table. The scene seems pretty normal except the silverware--each utensil is three feet long. In observing the scene, we see that nothing is happening; nobody is eating. Instead of eating all of those at table are fighting with each other. The utensils are so big that one cannot feed him or herself. Chaos is the result.

The image of heaven begins with the same banquet table. The meal is prepared; the people are present. Again, the silverware utensils are three feet long. All in heaven are eating, however. These people have learned that the only way they can eat is by feeding each other. Mutual cooperation allows all to be fed.

This Asian tale says something very powerfully about our modern world and society. It seems to say that individual pursuit will land you in the wrong place. The tale tells us about the differences between those who find total fulfillment and satisfaction in self, as opposed to those who find fulfillment and satisfaction in God. Our world places many temptations in our path. There is the temptation to self-indulgence from food, drink or drugs. There is the temptation to total self-satisfaction in work or sport. There is also the temptation to complete self-reliance, the idea that we have no need for others. It is the mentality that says I can do it all myself. Such individual pursuit is the Asian image of hell.

Scripture speaks to us about the need to channel our efforts away from self and toward the one thing that is truly valuable in our lives, namely God. In Matthew's Gospel (14:13-21) we hear the famous story of the feeding of the 5000. Jesus realizes that the people are hungry, but he also knows that their hunger is more than physical; it is one that has its roots in self-centeredness. The people have in certain important ways lost the true meaning of life.

Jesus, in his efforts to feed the people, shows that their efforts must be channeled toward and centered in God. It is important to note who feeds the crowd; it is not Jesus. Rather, we read that Jesus "broke the loaves and gave them to the disciples, and the disciples gave them to the crowds." (14:19b) Jesus teaches the apostles a lesson that they must feed the people; we must feed on another. Jesus goes even further. To assure that any effort toward God should not go unnoticed, all the fragments, twelve wicker baskets full, are gathered up so that no effort will be wasted.

In a similar way Isaiah, writing to the Hebrews in exile in Babylon (55:1-3), tells the people that they spend money, time and effort on what fails to satisfy. One can work 24 hours per day 7 days per week for oneself and never satiate our needs. In the process we forget about others and even God. Working for oneself can never fully satisfy one's need for God.

The words of Isaiah can be applied to us as well. We work hard for ourselves which is certainly necessary in this day and age. However, sometimes we lose our focus and in our own personal efforts we fail to see the needs of others; we fail to feed those around us. There is only one way to be satisfied--through God--everything else is empty and incomplete. We spend too much time concerned with the temporary, namely ourselves, that we at times neglect the time that must be spent in our relationship with God. Let us not forget God's words as spoken by Isaiah, "Listen carefully to me and eat what is good." (55:2b)

We need to respond to God, as God feeds us. We do this by feeding God's people. We feed others most profoundly by living lives of service and ministry, lives to which all the baptized are called. We also feed others by learning how to better love, both God and God's people. In order to love others, we must first know that God loves us. If there should be any doubt about this reality, we only need to listen to St. Paul when writing to the Romans: "Who will separate us from the love of Christ? Will hardship or distress or persecution or famine or nakedness or peril or sword? ... For I am convinced that neither death, nor life, nor Angels, nor rulers, nor things present, nor things to come, nor powers, nor height nor depth, nor anything else in all creation will be able to separate us from the love of God in Christ Jesus our Lord." (Romans 8:35, 38-39)

It is essential in our efforts to feed others that we keep our priorities straight. God must be number one in our lives; we must never waver or deviate from this tradition. Family and loved ones must be our second priority. All other things, such as work, relaxation, personal achievement must be somewhere down the line. If personal achievement or work come before God than they cannot be centered in him. Failure will be the result.

We need to get excited about God in our lives. We do this by going outside of ourselves in our efforts to help. Placing our own needs and desires behind those of others is something we are called to do in order to follow the Lord. Certainly, we need to be concerned about ourselves; in our society few will do it for us. But if we can channel our efforts so that all may benefit, then we can experience a greater sense of community and faith, and in the process, God is fed.

We come to Mass each Sunday to be fed at the Table of the Lord. We need to leave our cares, our personal "baggage" at the front door so as to fully enter into the celebration, so that God can feed us. God's feeding us can in turn get us involved, aid us to discover greater faith, and feed God's people in the process. Let us take the Asian image of heaven seriously and feed each other in imitation of Jesus, the source of all that is good.

Questions to Ponder:

1. What have I done recently to feed others, physically, emotionally, or spiritually?
2. How have I experienced God reaching out his hand to me, through the actions of our brothers and sisters?
3. When was the last time I went out of my way to spend time with someone, but I felt I had no time to spare?
4. How do I manifest my role as a Christian to be brother or sister to those who stand on the margins of our society?
5. When was the last time I had the courage to feed others with God's word by standing up for what I believe?

It's Never Too Late

We are all familiar with the term late-bloomers. It refers to people who respond later in life to an invitation and manage in the end to accomplish great things. History has known some famous late bloomers. Fortunately for us, early or late they followed the special invitation offered by God.

Anton Bruckner was a late bloomer. Many people do not know the name of Bruckner, but those who listen to classical music certainly know him. Bruckner lived in Austria in the late 19th century; he worked as a butcher and part-time organist. He was a very simple man. He always cut his hair very short, unusual for the time, and wore old clothes so as not to be mistaken for a person of wealth. Although his life was simple it was full. Yet, at the age of 41 he heard a performance of Richard Wagner's famous opera "Tristan and Isolde." The experience transformed his life. He decided to quit his job and dedicate himself to musical composition. By the end of his life he had completed, among many other works, nine symphonies, at least three of which are still regularly played by orchestras around the world.

The world knows Albert Einstein as a genius in the field of science. This is certainly true, but he did not start out that way. As a boy growing up in Germany many people thought him to be ignorant. He failed courses in mathematics; he was very rebellious. As a boy he showed little evidence of the ability he possessed. Yet, it was Einstein's Theory of Relativity and similar ideas which brought about the nuclear age in which we now live.

St. Augustine, one of the most brilliant Christian minds and greatest saints who ever lived, was also a late bloomer. Augustine wandered about for 30 years trying to find himself. He tried different religions including paganism and the religion of the holy man Mani, known today as Manichaeism. He was involved in a relationship and fathered a son. Eventually, through the prayers of his mother, St. Monica, he was converted to Christianity. St. Augustine's response to his conversion is a given in a famous line from his autobiography, *The Confessions*, "Late have I loved you,

O Beauty ever ancient, ever new, late have I loved you!" Augustine became a bishop and a great scholar. He was one of the most famous men who ever lived.

Each of these men received an invitation. One invitation was to music, another was to science. The third was an invitation to greater service of God. These invitations were always present, because they were gifts from God. Once the gift was found it became a permanent part of who these people were.

In Matthew's gospel (20:1-16), Jesus tells a parable that, while familiar to many is equally disturbing to many in contemporary life. We hear of how a landowner who hires people to work his vineyard. The invitation comes at different times, early in the morning, late in the afternoon, or sometime in between. Whenever the invitation is received, however, the reward is the same. Our natural reaction, created by our society, is confusion or anger. "It is not fair we say - equal work for equal pay." Such an attitude, although normal, misses the principal point of the story. Jesus wants us to know that God's invitation to join him is always present; it is never too late to say yes and accept the invitation.

It is difficult for us in today's society to accept such an attitude, an attitude of love. But Isaiah can help us to understand better. The prophet proclaims God's word to the Hebrews in exile, saying, "For as the heavens are higher than the earth, so are my ways higher than your ways and my thoughts than your thoughts." (Isaiah 55:9) In other words, God's ways are not human ways. God's ways and thoughts are above those of humans. God does no injustice at all in showing mercy to others. We are all given the opportunity; acceptance is our choice.

It is never too late for us! All of us have received many invitations from the Lord. Sometimes we have accepted God's invitation. Some invitations are still awaiting our response. And yes, sometimes we have passed by or even openly rejected the invitations of God. The invitation may have been too challenging, too difficult, or possibly we were not ready for it.

Scripture challenges us to accept God's invitation this day. The invitation may take many forms; its content could be one of many things. Maybe the invitation is to make your First Communion, be confirmed or married in the Church - it is never too late. Maybe the invitation is to accept a new direction in life, a path which may be uncertain, but one that is filled with possibilities - it is never too late. Maybe the invitation is to participate more fully in the life of the community of faith we share through service to our sisters and brothers - it is never too late. Maybe the invitation is to rediscover your relationship with another - yes, it is never too late. Maybe, yes just maybe, the invitation is to renew our personal relationship with God through prayer, ministry or contemplation -it is never too late.

      The invitation of the Lord is given this day. God's generosity is always unbelievable. But as Isaiah says, God's ways are above our ways. Let us accept God's invitation in whatever form it comes. Like Bruckner, Einstein or St. Augustine we may be late bloomers, but then in God's eyes it is never too late. Let us accept God's invitation and return to the Lord, the source of all that is good.

Questions to Ponder:

1. When was the last time I let an opportunity pass by because I felt I was not ready, able or sufficiently committed?
2. Why do I have difficulty, at times, with people who "get it wrong the first time?" How can I develop greater patience in dealing with such individuals?
3. How have I dealt with late bloomers in my family, at work or other situations in life?
4. Why do I think that my timetable is always the proper one? Can I learn to accept that God's timetable is better than mine?
5. When invitations from God have come my way, to go a different direction or to do something I find challenging, how have I reacted?

Setting a "Straight" Example

An old man lay dying in the hospital. As he wandered in and out of consciousness he began to speak. At the outset it seemed that his words were incoherent, but with time they began to make sense. It seems that something had happened long ago, something with consequences; he seemed very worried. His son was in the room and asked his father what was troubling him so much. The old man related a story from his youth. Is seems that one night he and some friends went to the main intersection, the crossroads of the town and, and just as a prank, decided to change the direction signs which pointed to the various communities in the area. Now so many years later he was gravely concerned about how many people he had led astray, how many had gone in the wrong direction because of him.

A man had a dream. In his vision he saw his son, the apple of his eye, who was gaily skipping, walking, and at times running down a well-lighted path. He did not seem to have a care in the world. Suddenly, without warning, the boy veered sharply off to the right onto a narrow and dark lane. The father could no longer see his son. From the darkness came a voice, the voice of his son: "Dad, you never showed me the correct path, and now I am lost." The man awoke, shaken by the dream, but glad that he could still do something about it.

Two short tales or vignettes but with one important and challenging message--what we do is vitally important. Our example either brings people closer to God or pushes them further away; people are not neutral on us. We have the challenge, therefore, to always direct people along the right path that leads to life with God.

Malachi the prophet was a man who understood the importance of setting a good example. He wrote to the Hebrew people upon returning from fifty years of exile in Babylon. Their nation is in disarray; the Temple, their central place of worship, lay in ruins. The people, uncertain as to where to turn, go to their former leaders for guidance. But Malachi criticizes the Hebrew leaders for their failures in the past. It was because these leaders led the people astray that they were sent into exile. We hear: "But you have turned aside from the way; you have caused many to stumble by your instruction; you have corrupted the covenant of Levi, says the Lord of hosts, and so I make you despised and abased before all the people, inasmuch as you have not kept my ways but have shown partiality in your instruction." (Malachi 2:8-9) The people have violated the covenant and transgressed the Mosaic Law because the leaders have not done what God asked of them.

Jesus, like Malachi, chastises the religious leaders of his day: "The scribes and the Pharisees sit on Moses' seat; therefore, do whatever they teach you and follow it; but do not do as they do, for they do not practice what they teach." (Matthew 23:2-3) The scribes and Pharisees have said all the right words, but their actions have been inconsistent with what they have said. The scribes and Pharisees have placed themselves over the people; they have separated themselves from all others. The people have been led astray because of the inconsistency between word and action. Because the religious leaders have made themselves better and separate from others, Jesus warns them of the consequences of their action: "All who exalt themselves will be humbled, and all who humble themselves will be exalted." (Matthew 23:12)

Setting a good example is very important. We know that it is one of the pillars of our common vocation to holiness. Fortunately, we have been blessed with many people in our lives who have set good example, people who have demonstrated a positive attitude and the shown us the correct direction. When we were in school, we met many teachers and coaches who opened whole new vistas to us. They inspired us to do our best and to never settle for less than 100% effort. They challenged us and were tough; but we received the message and were placed on the correct path. We have been blessed with people even closer to us-- parents, grandparents, Godparents, other family members, neighbors, and colleagues at work. These people too have shown us good example and placed us on the proper path.

Unfortunately, we have also experienced people who have led us astray. They have pushed us aside because of who we are-- our race, color, religious background or way of thinking. At times as well, we have been repulsed by what we observe or hear from others, observing an inconsistency in what others say and do. In our daily walk to draw closer to God we have become stagnant or maybe even reversed direction. The religious leaders during the time of Malachi and Jesus were not consistent in their actions and words. St. Paul, however, was faithful to his call. He gave a good example by working hard, day and night, so as not to impose on anyone (I Thessalonians 2:7-9).

We have a responsibility, as parents and children, as teachers and students, as professionals and office workers, as God's people, the Church, to set a good example, one that invites others to join us in the daily work of building the Kingdom of God in our world. We must not change the signposts in another's life and send that person in the wrong direction, as did the old man in the hospital. We must never abdicate our responsibility to be present to people and to show them the correct path, whether it be a spouse, a child, relative, neighbor, co-worker or even someone we barely know. People look to us for guidance; they listen to our words and observe our actions. Let us never disappoint them.

The challenge placed before us can be described in a comical but illustrative story. A teacher in a religious education class decided one day to begin the lesson by describing Jesus to her young students. "There is a man," she began, "who I would like you to meet. He is kind and compassionate. He loves everyone. He is always ready to help, and he is the best listener. All you have to do is speak and he will hear you. He will always direct you along the correct path; he is the type of person you want to follow." As the teacher spoke, there was a little girl in the back of the classroom wildly waving her hand seeking the teacher's recognition. But before the teacher could call upon her, the child's enthusiasm got the best of her and she burst out, "I know who you are talking about. He's my next-door neighbor." May we be so fortunate that someone, after observing what we do and hearing what we say, would say the same thing about us!

Questions to Ponder:

1. How have I, either consciously or unconsciously sent people in the wrong direction by my words and actions?
2. How do I understand my responsibility, as a follower of Christ, to bring his message to the world?
3. When people observe what I do and hear what I say, what is the message they receive?
4. How have I reacted when others, by their words and/or actions, push people further away from Christ? Do I have the courage to offer tough love in response?
5. In our contemporary world, what does it mean to set an example that is consistent with the message and mission of Jesus?

Sharing the Message of Christ

They called her "Sister" and to many thousands who jammed the Angelus Temple in Los Angeles on a regular basis to hear her preach she was that and more. Aimee Semple McPherson, one of the most famous Pentecostal preachers of the twentieth century was not one who took her task lightly. She did not consider her ministry one that she could take or leave; she was compelled to preach the Gospel and she did it quite well.

McPherson was born in Canada in 1890 and raised in a strict evangelical Protestant household. Her parents were active in the Salvation Army and thus, when she was ready to make her mark in the promotion of God's kingdom, she migrated toward the work of her parents. She married, immigrated to the United States and began an evangelistic career that saw her crisscross the country and go to China in her efforts to proclaim Christ's message. In 1919 she became an ordained minister in the Assemblies of God faith and began to tour the country in a series of revivals that modeled the famous frontier camp revivals in the early years of nineteenth century America. In 1923 she founded the Angeles Temple in Los Angeles which became the base for her Foursquare Gospel Church. In Los Angeles, near Hollywood, it was natural to become involved with religious radio programming as one of that medium's earliest pioneers.

Aimee was a natural at what she did, and people were attracted to her evangelistic message. For her evangelization and especially preaching was a compulsion. She had been called by God and responded using the gifts and talents she was given by the Lord.

The career of Aimee Semple McPherson is a good example of the evangelistic tradition in American Christianity. People like Billy Graham, Bishop Fulton Sheen, Father Patrick Peyton and Sinclair Lewis' famous protagonist, Elmer Gantry, are part of this rich tradition. In all these examples, evangelization was not something that people thought a good idea, but rather was a requirement for those privileged to live the Christian vocation. Scripture challenges us as followers of Jesus to be contemporary evangelists bringing others closer to Christ by all we do and say each and every day.

      Jesus was, of course, Christianity's first and foremost evangelist, the one upon whom all can model their call to proclaim the word. Mark 1: 35-39 describes how Jesus sets out with his disciples to initiate his public ministry. After preparing by prayer, and with the certainty that his notoriety and fame were spreading rapidly, Jesus tells his followers that he must be off to the neighboring village to proclaim the word there as he has done in Capernaum. Jesus was on a mission from his Father, to proclaim liberty to captives, release to prisoners and to declare a year of favor of the Lord. (Luke 4:18-19) He gathered a cadre of loyal followers, the apostles, who were his inner circle. But many others joined him, received the word, and went forward to continue his work.

      Premier among those not in the immediate inner circle was St. Paul, who as we recall, saw the risen Lord on the road to Damascus and was converted from being a great persecutor to a staunch evangelist for the new Christian way. This task, his mission and vocation, was not something Paul chose. On the contrary, God chose Paul for this work. As he tells the Corinthians (I Corinthians 9:16) a community he knew well, "If I proclaim the gospel, this gives me no ground for boasting, for an obligation is laid on me, and woe to me if I do not proclaim the gospel." He expects no recompense for his efforts. His only concern is that the message is being proclaimed. Paul became all things to all people in order to save a few. He proclaims the Gospel confident that he will share in its blessings.

      As baptized Christians we have been called to be evangelists, to preach God's word to others. This vocation will not be easy and should not be taken lightly, for it is part of our mission as followers of Jesus. We might think, like Job (7:7-8) proclaims, "My days are swifter than a weaver's shuttle, and come to their end without hope. Remember that my life is a breath; my eye will never again see good. The eye that beholds me will see me no more." For Job, life is drudgery and pain and we seem to have no reason to proclaim the word to others, but we cannot avoid our responsibilities. Paul tells his friend Timothy in the Scriptures "I solemnly urge you: proclaim the message; be persistent when the time is favorable or unfavorable; convince, rebuke, and encourage, with the utmost patience in teaching." (II Timothy 4:1c-2) We, like Jesus and St. Paul, are compelled to be evangelists and to proclaim the word. We can proclaim the word in a vast assembly like Aimee Semple McPherson, Billy Graham or Patrick Peyton, but most of us do so every day in the ordinary and even mundane actions and encounters of life. When we smile, the world smiles. When we say, "Have a good day," the world says the same. When we demonstrate the love and goodness of Christ to others in word and deed, the world will be made a better place. The Christian vocation to holiness and service beckons us to fall in line with the great men and women of history who have proclaimed with their lives the message of Christ. Let us be aware of our common vocation to be evangelists, to bring others to Jesus. It is the Lord whom we serve; it is the eternal life he promised that will be our reward!

Questions to Ponder:

1. How do I understand my vocation as a Christian to preach the gospel to others?
2. When conversations arise that present the opportunity to present the Christian perspective what has been my response?
3. What is the message that people receive when they hear my words and observe my actions? Am I following the message of Jesus or presenting an alternative to others?
4. What has been my response when I hear or observe others who seek to tear down rather than build up the Kingdom of God?
5. Why at times do I deny or push aside my responsibility to preach the gospel to others?

Discipleship: Being All You Can Be

There once was a young man who decided to become a saint. He left his home, family, and possessions, gave everything to the poor and walked out into the desert to find God. Eventually in the desert he found a cave. He thought to himself, "Here I will be alone with God; there is nothing to distract me." He prayed day and night in the cave, but he still received great temptations. He imagined all the good things of life that he wanted desperately, but he was determined to meet his goal and to have God alone. After many months the temptations stopped, and St. Anthony of the Desert was at peace having nothing but God.

However, according to legend, God told Anthony, "Leave your cave for a few days and go to a distant town. Look there for the town shoemaker and stay with him and his family." The holy hermit was puzzled by God's command, but nonetheless left the next morning. After a long walk he arrived in the distant town. After some inquiries he found the shoemaker's home. He knocked on the door and asked, "Are you the town shoemaker?" The young man said he was and invited the hermit to enter his humble home. The shoemaker called his wife. Together the two invited Anthony to stay with them, providing him a clean and safe place to stay and wonderful meals. During his stay the hermit asked the shoemaker and his wife all sorts of questions about their lives, but he revealed very little about his own, even though the couple was very curious. Over those few days the three became good friends.

After three days the hermit bid goodbye to the couple. He walked back to his cave wondering why God had asked him to make this visit. When he arrived home, God asked Anthony, "What was the shoemaker like?" The hermit responded, "He is a simple man. He lives with his wife who is now pregnant. They love each other very much. They have a very simple life, and both work very hard. They give money and food to those who have less than they have. They pray at least once each day and enjoy each other's company very much." God listened carefully to Anthony's words and responded, "You will be a great saint, Anthony, but so too will be the shoemaker and his wife."

This story says something of great importance about being a follower of Christ, that is being a disciple. It's not about who we are or precisely what we do; rather discipleship is all about our faithfulness in carrying out our vocation whatever it may be. Many passages in Scripture challenge us to be good disciples, realizing that being a follower of Jesus will not be easy, but will be worth every ounce of our effort.

During his public ministry Jesus gathered around him an inner circle of 12 apostles and many other unnamed disciples. He taught them and demonstrated by his actions how they were to live their lives. In Luke 9:21b-22 Jesus presents a difficult challenge to his disciples by foreshowing his own suffering and death: "The Son of Man must undergo great suffering, and be rejected by the elders, chief priests, and scribes and be killed:" Jesus is very clear that discipleship is not about saving your life now, but rather losing it for others so that you may find life eternal: "If any want to become my followers, let them deny themselves and take up their cross daily and follow me. For those who want to save their life will lose it, and those who live lose their life for my sake will save it." (Luke 9:23b-24)

What Jesus told his followers was the fulfillment of what the prophet Zechariah (12:10) had told the people of Judah many centuries earlier: "And I will pour out a spirit of compassion and supplication on the house of David and the inhabitants of Jerusalem, so that, when they look on the one whom they have pierced, they shall mourn for him, as one mourns for an only child, and weep bitterly over him, as one weeps over a firstborn." Thus, not only does Jesus fulfill the prophecy, but he challenges us to fulfill our Christian duty and be willing to suffer so others may have something of the abundance of God.

How can we be disciples in our contemporary world? The story of Anthony, the shoemaker, and his wife is a clear indication that discipleship means being faithful. We might go to the desert as did Anthony or we may live a simple life as the family. We may make headlines in the papers for scientific discoveries or special accomplishments, be a person who works at the local grocery or hardware store, serve as an administrative or clerical person in an office, be a student at school, or service customers at a local bank. Discipleship is not about what we do, but it is everything about who we are and how we carry out our daily responsibilities. The Army recruiting slogan, "Be all that you can be," is a succinct and poignant way to synthesize the Christian vocation be a follower of Christ. This will not be easy, and if we live our lives well it will involve suffering. Again, as Jesus says we must pick up our cross daily and follow in his footsteps. We must not shy away or seek to avoid pain, but rather meet our responsibilities, whatever they may be, head-on.

Yes, there is no one formula to become a saint and there is no one way to be a follower of Jesus. But we must be willing to give everything. A humorous little story illustrates my point. One day President Dwight Eisenhower, speaking at the National Press Club, apologized to the reporters saying that he felt he wasn't much of an orator. It reminded him of his boyhood on a Kansas farm. There was a farmer, the President related, who owned a dairy cow that Eisenhower's father wanted to buy. He asked the farmer about the cow's pedigree, but the old man didn't know what that meant. So, Mr. Eisenhower asked the farmer about the cow's butterfat production. But the farmer said he had no idea about that either. Finally, Mr. Eisenhower asked the farmer if he knew how many gallons of milk the cow produced each month. By now the farmer was puzzled, shook his head and said "I don't know. But one thing I do know for sure is that she's an honest old cow and she will give you all the milk she has." Let us give God all that we have, our time, talent, and opportunities. Let us recommit ourselves today to being full-time disciples of Jesus Christ.

Questions to Ponder:

1. What does it mean to me to be a saint? How can I manifest "saintly behavior" in my life?
2. Why at times do I hold back and not give my full effort to various endeavors? What am I trying to save or avoid?
3. Why do some people's approaches to God make me mad or nervous?
4. When God calls me unexpectedly, as he called Anthony, what has been my reaction?
5. How charitable has my response been when God calls me to share my time, talent, and treasure with others in need?

Discipleship Requires Commitment

One day the local pastor at the Catholic Church in town received a call from a man who wanted to join the parish. The man was very eager, but he went on to explain to the priest that he had some stipulations to his membership. He said that he did not want anyone to force him to attend Mass every week, study the Bible, be an usher, or visit the sick. Above all, he would not be a Eucharistic minister, a lector and certainly not a religious education teacher. The pastor commended the man for his desire to become a member of the parish, but he told him that the parish he really wanted to join was across town. He gave the caller the directions and then politely hung up the phone. The man got into his car and followed the pastor's directions to the letter. When he arrived, he immediately came face-to-face with the logical conclusions from his own apathetic attitude. There stood an old abandoned church, boarded up and ready for demolition.

One day a businessman was asked by a reporter, "What is your occupation?" He answered, "I am a Christian." But the newspaper man continued, "No, what is your job?" The reply was the same, "I am a Christian." "You don't understand," pressed the reporter. "What do you do for a living?" "Listen," said the businessman, "my full-time job in being a Christian; however, I own a furniture store to pay the bills."

Some years ago, deep sea divers located a 400-year old sunken ship off the coast of Ireland. Among the treasures they found onboard was a man's wedding ring. When it was cleaned up, the divers noticed that the ring had an inscription on it. Etched on the wide band were two hands holding a heart. Under the etching were the words, "I have nothing more to give you." Of all the treasures on that sunken ship none moved the divers more than the ring and its beautiful inscription.

Three short vignettes that have one common and powerful theme--commitment. To be committed means to refuse to count the cost, but rather to fully and willingly engage in the life of discipleship.

Calculating the cost of discipleship, the price of being a follower of Jesus, is something that must be done, but we often avoid this task because of its possible ramifications for our lives. Scripture presents this challenge as clearly as the three short stories. In Luke's Gospel (14:25-33), Jesus says that nothing can come before God--not family, friends, not even oneself. The Lord is very clear, "Whoever does not carry the cross and follow me cannot be my disciple." (14:27) Dietrich Bonheoffer, a famous mid-20th century Lutheran pastor and theologian, said in his famous book *The Cost of Discipleship*, that to be a disciple of the Lord would cost us our lives. Before we can pick up the cross and be disciples, however, we, if prudent, must calculate the cost; we must prepare for the commitment that we make. If we fail to take this important step, we most likely will never make it to our goal-- that is eternal life with God. Jesus in the Gospel provides two examples of pre-calculation and preparation--building a tower and preparing for battle. In the story of the tower the person tries to prevent a folly, his own ridicule by others, if he cannot finish the project. The king must never enter into battle unless through prior calculation he is confident that victory can be secured. The point of these examples is not to show that there is an option in following or not following Christ. We are all called to be disciples. However, we must prepare; we must be committed.

Our preparation for discipleship should not, however, lead us to believe that we cannot do it, that the cost is too high. The author of the Book of Wisdom (9:13-18) tells us that often we as finite and, therefore, limited humans often shortchange ourselves, not giving ourselves the opportunity to show what we can do. Such an attitude unknowingly short circuits God and the Lord's ability, but Wisdom reminds us that God cannot be so limited. We must trust that God can and will give us the strength, courage, patience, and any other gifts necessary to calculate the outlay, take up the cross, and be true disciples of Christ.

All of us can site numerous examples in our lives of how we have planned out projects to assure that we can complete them satisfactorily. It may have been the construction of a fence around our property, or the financing of a new car, remodeling our home, or a child's college education. If we spend so much time calculating these important matters of our life, should we not take an even greater interest and, therefore, amount of time in planning our relationship with the Lord? Do we understand that while the gift of eternal life is free, we must figure our level of commitment? We cannot get to our destination on a trip via plane, train or car without planning. Can we expect to reach God without giving it sufficient thought, time, and energy?

Because the cost of discipleship is so great, because it will cost us everything, we need to turn now to our source of strength. Again, as the Book of Wisdom tells us the sustenance we need for this journey is God's wisdom, which straightens out the often crooked paths that humans take. We read, "For who can learn the counsel of God? Or who can discern what the Lord wills?" (9:13) Seeking the wisdom of God, that wisdom so far beyond us, can allow us to calculate the cost of what our relationship with Christ will be. This faith will allow us to take up the cross, making the Lord the ultimate destination of our journey.

The businessman who was a full time Christian and the inscription on the man's ring challenge us to seek greater commitment in our life. Scripture challenges us to properly prepare and to calculate the cost of our commitment. Let us plan now so that we can complete our journey, to Christ and eternal life.

Questions to Ponder:

1. What am I willing to pay to be a true disciple of Jesus Christ?
2. When was the last time I took the time to calculate what the cost of my discipleship might be?
3. When I have been in positions to stand up for what the faith teaches, what has been my response?
4. How do I manifest my commitment to my family, responsibilities, and especially to God?
5. How have I carried out Jesus' great challenge to lay down my life for my friends? What more can I do?

Never Counting the Cost

"When Christ calls a man, he bids him to come and die." These words were written by Dietrich Bonhoeffer, a well-known Lutheran pastor and theologians, in a book influential to many, *The Cost of Discipleship*, first published in 1937. Bonhoeffer lived his Christian call to holiness without counting the cost. He did what God asked of him and he did it without qualification, reservation or question. He did not look over his shoulder and wonder why, but rather lived what he wrote. Discipleship, if lived fully, would cost him his life.

Bonhoeffer was born in the state of Prussia in 1906. He grew up in an academic environment near the University of Berlin where his father was a professor of neurology and psychiatry. Later in his own study of theology he became interested in the historical-critical method of Adolph von Harnack and was a disciple of Swiss theologian Karl Barth who promoted the new "theology of revelation." After completing his doctorate, Bonhoeffer spent 1931 at New York's Union Theological Seminary in a post-doctorate fellowship and exchange program. Returning to Germany he resumed duties which he had earlier begun as a pastor and writer.

In 1933, however, things changed for Bonhoeffer, the German people, and ultimately the world with the rise of the Nazi regime and Adolph Hitler. Bonhoeffer was one of the first and most vocal opponents of the Nazi ideology of anti-Semitism. Between 1935 and 1940 Bonhoeffer headed an underground seminary for Germany's "Confessing Church," (even though it was proscribed in 1937) which led the German Protestant resistance to Hitler. He was able to continue his work as pastor and theologian in the early war years under cover as a member of the military intelligence community. Bonhoeffer believed that the root evil for many of society's problems was a lax attitude toward morality which he said was fostered by the ready availability of "cheap grace" to members of the Church. He was an ecumenist and promoted his belief in his speeches and writings.

In April 1943, because of his books, essays, and talks, Bonhoeffer was arrested for insurrection. He was imprisoned, but this only strengthened his beliefs. It was at this time that he wrote his most famous work, *Prisoner of God: Letters and Papers from Prison*. Implicated in a failed July 1944 plot to assassinate Hitler, Bonhoeffer was transferred to a concentration camp at Flossenberg in Bavaria where on April 9, 1945, only days before the allied liberation of the camp, he was executed. Dietrich Bonhoeffer died for the Christian beliefs which formed his life; he was a martyr who never counted the cost.

Christianity is a commitment and like Dietrich Bonhoeffer, we are called to that fullness of discipleship. We, too, cannot count the cost. Jesus certainly knew this and he tried to tell his apostles and those other disciples that the cost of discipleship would be one's whole life. In the Gospel of Luke (9:51-62) Jesus encounters three different people on his way to Jerusalem and his salvific death for all of us. The first person tells Jesus that he will follow him wherever he goes. The Lord's response is somewhat confusing and metaphorical: "Foxes have holes, and birds of the air have nests; but the Son of Man has nowhere to lay his head." (9:58) Jesus is saying that one might follow, but it is necessary to give welcome to Jesus first. A second person requests permission to bury his father. Jesus' answer is short and to the point, "Let the dead bury their own dead; but as for you, go and proclaim the kingdom of God." (9:60) A third person requests to take leave of his family. Jesus' response is general yet powerful, "No one who puts a hand to the plow and looks back is fit for the kingdom of God." (9:62) In other words Jesus is saying that if one wishes to follow, to be a disciple, then it is necessary for one to be fully committed. A discipleship of reservation is not what Jesus asks; we must never count the cost.

This idea of total commitment was not foreign to the Jewish people. Elisha, the young protégé of Elijah the prophet was committed to his mentor (I Kings 19:16-21). He never wanted to leave Elijah's side. The commitment which Jesus asks of us is in service to God, which is generally carried out in ministry to God's people. Writing to the Christian community in Galatia, St. Paul puts it this way: "Live by the Spirit, I say, do not gratify the desires of the flesh." (Galatians 5:16)

God calls us each day to be disciples--what has been our response? The first commitment in faith we made was at our baptism. (Galatians 5:16)

We committed ourselves at that time to lead lives of holiness, to be servants and disciples. As our life journey continues our commitments change; they are different during the various stages of life. But one thing is certain, our Christian commitment must be total; we cannot count the cost. For young people the commitment can be found in education and family. As we know, education is a priceless gift. If students are not committed, then they run the risk of missing the opportunity of a lifetime and destroying potential before it has the opportunity to blossom. Education requires students to be single-minded; they cannot be worried or concerned about what others think or do. Young people must also be committed to their families--taking responsibility when it is asked and being obedient when it is required.

When we become adults our commitments shift. We must be committed to our place of work. A just wage requires our honest and full effort. We must always work in an ethical manner and reject short-cuts or other practices which may threaten or compromise our Christian values and principles. Most adults find commitment in marriage, to love unconditionally and without reservation. All of us as well must be committed to our community, to give back to the world in some measure to make it a better place now and in the future.

Christian commitment must be complete and certainly such a challenge is not easy--but then most good things in life require our sincere efforts. Commitment is an action of the heart, not the head. We might give of our financial resources, time, and expertise, but if we do so only as an act of the head, then we will have reservations and qualifications and constantly be looking over our shoulder and asking questions; we will always be counting the cost. However, if our actions are of the heart, then our commitment will be complete, and we will experience the fullness of discipleship.

      Dietrich Bonhoeffer was a man who lived and died according to the Christian principles which he learned as a youth and fostered and proclaimed as an adult. In the face of conflict, even the political and theological absence of God preached by Nazism, he continued to hold fast. He never counted the cost, even when the price was his very life. Jesus asks us, as he did his servant Dietrich Bonhoeffer, to be totally committed as Christians. Such devotion takes courage, but it is possible. As a loving mother stands in a pool with her arms outstretched just waiting for her child, who stands on the edge of the pool frightened and crying, to jump in, so Jesus is always present with his arms spread wide asking us to have the courage to take the risk and be committed Christians. "When Christ calls a man, he bids him to come and die." Let us always manifest the courage to never count the cost of discipleship. Let us demonstrate what we believe.

Questions to Ponder:

1. How far am I willing to go to manifest my belief in Christ?
2. Why do I periodically count the cost of my discipleship? Why do I hold back in my relationship with the Lord?
3. What does it mean to me to be a disciple of Jesus in the 21st century?
4. What areas of my life require that I re-commit myself—family, friends, work, God?
5. How do I react when others are not as committed as they should be? Do I have the courage to challenge the person?

Persistence Rewarded

History records the expression, *Athanasius contra mundum*--Athanasius against the world. These words aptly express the situation in the fourth century Church when heresy almost reigned supreme--save Athanasius, a bishop who was a persistent and staunch defender of the Faith. Athanasius was born into a Christian family in Alexandria, Egypt in 295 AD. In his early twenties he was ordained and entered the service of Alexander, Bishop of Alexandria. He accompanied the bishop to the first ecumenical council of the Church at Nicaea when, among other matters, the heresy of Arianism, which promoted the idea that Jesus was not God, was first condemned.

Three years later, in 328, Alexander died, and Athanasius was selected as the new bishop of Alexandria. It was at this time that his life as a persistent defender of the Faith began in earnest. His first opponent was Melitius, a fellow bishop, who believed that it was wrong for the Church to welcome back those who had apostatized. His greatest nemeses, however, were the Arians, who although condemned at Nicaea, continued to grow and attract many to their theological perspective. In fact, Arianism was so widespread that St. Jerome, the original translator of the Scriptures into Latin (the Vulgate), once famously wrote, "The world awoke and found itself Arian."

Between 335 and 366, as one of the few bishops in the Eastern Church who held the orthodox faith, Athanasius was exiled on five different occasions for a total of seventeen years. Trumped-up charges, false testimony, and the events of the day combined to work against him. But each time that he returned from exile he was that much more determined to defend the true Faith. During his exiles he wrote many important treatises, including *The Life of Anthony*, a biography of Anthony of the Desert, one of the first desert monks and a precursor to the monastic life. Through tenacity, perseverance, and the fact that he was able to outlive almost all his opponents, Athanasius, in the end, was able to prevail. He died in 373, living his last seven years in relative peace. His greatest triumph came, however, in 381 at the Council of Constantinople when the Nicene-Constantinopolitan Creed, the one professed each Sunday at Mass, was written and accepted. It was a testimony to Athanasius' persistence and dedication. He triumphed, became a saint, and inherited eternal life.

St. Athanasius' life provides a good example of the general idea of persistence, which is often described in the Scriptures. Abraham was certainly persistent, and one might think rather bold in a conversation he had with God over the fate of Sodom and Gomorrah (Genesis 18:20-32). Abraham challenged God's mercy and compassion. Clearly Abraham did not want any who were righteous to die with those who were evil as the Lord had threatened. Thus, through his persistence, Abraham was able to convince God, in a figurative sense, that the city should not be destroyed even if there were only ten righteous people present there.

In Luke's Gospel (11:5-13) Jesus tells the story of a man who is persistent in asking his neighbor for assistance. We are told that the favor is granted, not because of friendship, but as a result of the persistence of the one who is asking. Jesus, however, goes further and says we must be persistent as well in our requests to God. Jesus says, "Ask, and it will be given you; search, and you will find; knock, and the door will be opened for you. (11:9-10) Jesus will answer our prayers. The response might not come when we expect it or be of the nature we desire, but God will always meet our needs. We must remember, however, that sometimes our needs and our wants are not the same.

We need to be persistent in all that we do. Life, as we know, is filled with obstacles, some detours, and even some roadblocks. When these difficulties present themselves, we have two basic options. We can "throw in the towel," surrender, and say "we are defeated," or we can pick ourselves up, wipe off the dust and dirt, and continue along the road, finding a new route if necessary to get where we need and want to be.

Persistence in our life will eventually lead us home to God. We must be persistent in our daily work. Sometimes the poor work ethic and pettiness of others gets us down, but this is when we must be persistent to do what is right simply because it is right. We must also be persistent in what we do. We must work diligently at our tasks giving them our best effort. We also must be persistent in relationships. Marriage requires daily vigilance and much work for two to act as one. All relationships, however, require our perseverance. Sometimes our persistence means challenging people--family members, friends, colleagues--to move beyond where they presently find themselves to a new and higher plane. Sometimes persistence means demonstrating greater love and compassion toward others. Still other times persistence in relationships means providing a listening ear and being present to one who needs us. We must be persistent with God and God's people. We must never give up on another, for God never gives up on any of us. God pursues us, as Francis Thompson suggests in his poem, "The Hound of Heaven," constantly and without rest. We must bring ourselves to God in all respects.

    Athanasius was a persistent and staunch defender of the Faith. Lies, deceit, even exile could not deter him from his path. Certainly, he was knocked off stride on several occasions, but through his persistence he always returned to continue the path that leads to God. We must, like Athanasius, doggedly pursue our goals at work, in relationships, and especially with God. Let us, therefore, be persistent in all that we do; our reward in heaven will be great.

Questions to Ponder:

1. Why do I give up too easily on projects and people? Why do I find myself disappointed in others?
2. When adversity strikes and I am proverbially or literally forced to my knees, what has been my reaction?
3. How can I assist others who have given up on themselves or others?
4. When life throws me off stride and forces me to go in another direction, what has been my reaction?
5. God has never and will never give up on us. Why at times do I give up on God?

If You Really Love God--Show Me!

William Barclay, a famous commentator on Sacred Scripture, tells a story of an Orthodox Jewish rabbi who was imprisoned in a cruel regime. He was barely able to survive so meager were the rations of food and water that he was given. As an Orthodox Jew he scrupulously maintained the letter of the law in everything concerning dietary rules and cleanliness. Each day when he received his meager portion of food and water, he made certain that he made all the ritual washings before eating and he only ate those things that the law did not forbid. In the process he almost always used up his ration of drink in washing and nearly wasted away from the lack of food. Fortunately, he got out of prison in time, for if his time was any longer, he would have died of thirst and malnutrition--all of his own making!

There is a story told by a missionary in New Guinea. An old man who was a recent convert to Christianity came to the mission hospital every day to read the gospels to the patients. One day the man was having great difficulty reading. The doctor examined him and discovered that he was going blind and would probably be so in a year or two at most. After this revelation the old man was not found at the hospital; no one knew what had happened to him. Eventually one of the missionaries found him and brought the mission doctor to him. The old man explained that he had not come to the hospital because he was busy memorizing the gospels while he could still see. "Soon I'll be back at the hospital," he told the doctor, "and I will continue my work of teaching the gospel to the patients."

One day in 1942 a prisoner attempted to escape from the notorious Nazi death camp at Auschwitz in Poland. The camp commander, irritated at this bold action, decided to teach the other prisoners a sobering lesson. He selected ten men at random and scheduled them to be executed in public. One of the men selected was a family man, who had been befriended by a Franciscan priest, Maximilian Kolbe, who was also a prisoner. The priest stepped forward and offered to take the family man's place. The camp commander was stunned but accepted the offer. Maximilian Kolbe died so another might live and, in the process, carried out Jesus command, "Greater love than this no man hath, then to lay down one's life for a friend." (John 15:13)

These three stories all speak of the love of sacrifice, sacrifice of self to the law of God, and sacrifice of self for the needs and lives of others. Scripture challenges us to consider how much we love God and our neighbor and to demonstrate that love to all. God gave Moses, the great liberator of the Israelites, the Law, the stone tablets upon which were written the Ten Commandments. The Law was critical to the Hebrews for it formed their whole way of thinking and living. The importance of the Law was made clear by Moses: "Hear therefore, O Israel, and observe them [the Commandments] diligently, so that it may go well with you." (Deuteronomy 6:3a) The first and most important commandment was to love God with one's whole heart, soul, mind, and strength. Nothing was more important than this command for the Hebrews. In the Gospel of Mark, Jesus repeats Moses' words, but he goes one important step further. Jesus agrees that love of God with one's whole heart, mind, soul, and strength was fundamental, but in explicating "The Golden Rule" he says, "You shall love your neighbor as yourself." (Mark 12:31b)

Few would disagree with the challenge presented in the Scriptures; we would not be Christians if we did not love God and make an effort to love our neighbor, but how do we truly show we love God and our neighbor? To what length will we go to demonstrate what we say we believe as practicing Christians? In the Broadway musical "My Fair Lady" Eliza Doolittle becomes fed up with the protestations of love found in letters from her boyfriend Freddy and in her exasperation sings the song, "show Me!" She says that she is sick of words and talk. "If there is any love burning in your heart," she sings, "show me!" I believe God might ask the same thing of us. If we truly love God what are we doing to demonstrate that love to God and neighbor in concrete ways? The author of the Letter to the Hebrews tells us that Jesus loved us so much that he offered himself for us and constantly stands ready to intercede to the Father on our behalf (Hebrews

7:23-28). Are we ready to offer ourselves for God and our neighbor?

How have we truly demonstrated our love for God and God's people, our neighbors? When was the last time we supported someone who was being maligned or unjustly criticized in a conversation within our family or at work? How many times recently have we intentionally gone out of our way to assist another person, possibly at great personal risk or to the detriment of our own advancement? When you had the opportunity to defend God and/or the Church against the many attacks it daily receives from the media, anti-Catholics, even those within our fold who are angry, concerning issues like abortion and euthanasia, did you take the occasion seriously and make a case for God? Do we love God sufficiently that we will make daily prayer, weekly Mass, and regular celebration of the sacrament of penance normative in our lives and refuse to make excuses when we fail? Do we love God so much that we would have the courage to give up all we are and hope to be so that God's Kingdom may be advanced in our world?

The Golden Rule, to love God with our whole heart, soul, mind, and strength, and our neighbor as ourself, will be only a pious platitude unless we are ready to truly show God that we mean what we say. Let us, therefore, critically examine our lives and ask the hard question of what we have done lately to truly manifest in concrete ways our love for God. Our inner search may discover things we wish not to admit, but if we clear out the doubts and uncertainties then we can fill the void with new resolve to love beyond all measure and without counting the cost. Our reward will be eternal life.

Questions to Ponder:

1. What have I done lately to manifest the love of God to others I encounter on a daily basis?
2. How do I understand the meaning of sacrifice in my relations with others and with God?
3. Why do I find loving my neighbor so difficult? What inhibits my love for others?
4. What more must I sacrifice in order to truly say that I am a disciple of Jesus in all I say and do?
5. How have I reacted when others have not been loving toward me?

Part III: Essays on Ministry

Overview

The road to Jesus and eventually life eternal is never an easy path for it requires much of us along the way. Armed with faith and convinced of our need to be disciples, we must now enter into active ministry to assist God's people regardless of our vocation in life. After Jesus called both the original 12 and later the 72, he sent them out on mission. They were to go without many of the basic things that we today would consider essential. We would not even go for an overnight at a local hotel or visit with a family member or friend without packing a change of clothes, toiletries, and probably these days an electronic device or two. Yet, Jesus specifically told these first disciples: "Carry no purse, no bag, no sandals; and greet no one on the road. Whatever house you enter, first say, 'Peace to this house!' … Remain in the same house, eating and drinking whatever they provide, for the laborer deserves to be paid." (Luke 10:3-5, 7a)

As people of faith who are disciples of Jesus Christ, we have all been commissioned through baptism to do Christ's work in our world. Indeed, it is our responsibility to do what we can, dependent on our vocation in life, to preach Christ's word and to act in his name in building the Kingdom of God. Sometimes we mistakenly think that ministry is the purview of the clergy and religious alone, but this is far from the truth. All are called to serve, utilizing the gifts and talents provided by God to further the work initiated by Jesus. We can do this in many ways. We may speak to people and by such means bring some closer to Christ. However, as the expression goes, actions speak louder than words. Random acts of kindness can help to counter the random acts of violence that too often today plague our world. St. Francis of Assisi once famously stated, "Preach the gospel at all times and when necessary use words." Clearly, this famous Mendicant disciple of Jesus opted for action in his life and preached the same message to his fellow Franciscans.

The Christian faith we possess and the privilege that we have of being disciples of Jesus Christ must find its greatest manifestation in ministry to our brothers and sisters. Jesus initiated the Kingdom of God, but his work was not completed upon his return to the Father. The gravity and significance of our responsibility to apply our time, talent, and treasure for the betterment of God's people through ministry is made crystal clear in a little story: When Jesus ascended to heaven, following his resurrection and final instructions to his followers, he was greeted by the Father in heaven. After the Father warmly greeted his Son and welcomed him home, he asked, "Jesus, did you complete all the work I sent you into the world to accomplish?" Jesus responded, "Father, I only began the work; there is much more to be done." The Father then spoke to Jesus, "Son, who did you leave in charge and do you have confidence that they will do what you have asked them to do?" "Yes, Father," Jesus responded, "I left my apostles and disciples to do the work and I am confident that they will do well." "But, Jesus, what if they fail; what will happen if they do not carry out your mission? Do you have a backup plan?" Jesus responded, "No, Father, there is no backup plan. I am counting on them to get the job done." So, there is no backup plan; Jesus counting on us to do his work in our world. Let us not disappoint him!

Completing the Master's Work

Classical music provides some significant examples of great musical compositions that were never finished by their composers. A perennial favorite with many, Wolfgang Amadeus Mozart, never completed his magnificent Requiem Mass. Franz Schubert, who like Mozart lived only a short life, but produced over 600 works of music, wrote only two movements of his eighth symphony. Orchestras today still play this great composition, known as the "Unfinished Symphony." The best example, however, is the work of opera "superstar" Giacomo Puccini, who lived in the latter nineteenth and early twentieth centuries. Puccini also left a master creation unfinished, but, fortunately for the world his students, known as his disciples, finished their master's work.

Giacomo Puccini was in his day the star of the world of opera. He gained great fame, not only in his native land of Italy, but throughout the world. It was quite common to hear people along the streets of any great city whistling or humming one of the many popular melodies from such great works as Tosca, La Boheme, Madama Butterfly, Manon Lescaut, and Gianni Schicchi.

When he was in his 60s, Puccini took on a significant challenge, the composition of another great opera. The libretto told the story of a gallant young man, Calaf, in his efforts to win the hand in marriage of a stern, mysterious, and seemingly cold Chinese princess named Turandot. Puccini labored for four years, but he was a very sick man and he knew he was running out of time. Puccini returned home to God before his master work was completed. Because he was a famous man, Puccini had many friends, including a cadre of loyal students, known as his disciples. These young men and women could not bear the thought that their master's great work, his *magnum opus,* would lie unfinished. Thus, they gathered together, studied the score of the opera, and then when ready began the difficult task of finishing their master's work.

In 1926, two years after his death, Puccini's opera, "Turandot," considered by many opera lovers to be his best work, was performed for the first time, appropriately enough at Milan's La Scala Opera House with Arturo Toscanni, the most famous conductor of the day, at the podium. When the opera reached the point where Puccini's work ended Toscanni paused, set down his baton, and said, "Thus far the master wrote, but he died." After a moment of silence Toscanni again picked up his baton, turned to the audience, and with tears in his eyes said, "But his disciples finished his work." Thunderous applause was heard as the opera continued; the work of the master had been completed.

In some important ways Giacomo Puccini's life paralleled that of Jesus. Christ was sent by God to be with us for a certain amount of time; He was sent on a mission. Like Puccini, who was sent by God to delight our ears with beautiful music, so Jesus was sent to show us how to lead good and holy lives, to demonstrate the presence of God in the world. We know, however, that Jesus was not able to complete his mission, a reality that the Lord himself knew and, thus, as we recall, Jesus sent out many disciples two by two to do their best to complete their Master's work (Luke 10:1-12). Jesus was quite clear, "The harvest is plentiful, but the laborers are few; therefore, ask the Lord of the harvest to send out laborers into his harvest." (10:2) These disciples were sent with what Jesus knew they needed. They did not need money or extra clothing, the things people generally believe are necessary on journeys. No, Jesus sent them forward with the message of the prophet Isaiah. The great prophet wrote to the Hebrews who had just returned from fifty years of exile in Babylon and told them that God would bring prosperity to the people. He proclaimed, "I will extend prosperity to her like a river, and the wealth of the nations like an overflowing stream; ... As a mother comforts her child, so I will comfort you." (Isaiah 66: 12a, 13a) God promised to care for the people in as loving a manner as that of a woman sharing herself with an infant child. Jesus knew what was necessary to carry on his work and it was not the things of the world, but rather the things that only God can provide.

Jesus knew that the ministry would not be easy. In the same story of Jesus sending forth his disciples, we read, "See, I am sending you out like lambs in the midst of wolves." (Luke 10:3)

Thus, he armed the disciples with the greatest of all messages. He knew they would need to be dedicated.

In a similar way, St. Paul knew quite a bit about dedication. He wrote to the Galatians (6:14), "May I never boast of anything except the cross of our Lord Jesus Christ." To be a follower, to go out on mission, to do our share to complete the Master's work will lead us to the cross as well.

As the seventy-two were sent forward, so we a contemporary 21st century band of disciples are asked to go forward and do our share, shoulder the burden, in completing our Master's work. We go into an often-hostile world and sometimes we hesitate; we choose not to get involved. We often say, "O, ministry, that is for those who have the time or the talent; I will simply choose to follow and let others lead." Such an attitude is counterproductive; it does nothing to advance the cause of Christ in our world. If we are not going to do the work, who will? St. Teresa of Avila, the famous 16th century Carmelite mystic and religious reformer once wrote, "Christ has no body on earth, but yours, no hands or feet, but yours. Your's are the eyes through which Christ sees with compassion for the world. Christ has body on earth but your's."

Yes, Jesus is calling us to go forward. We have been trained and we have the requisite skills and knowledge; now we must develop the proper attitude. Giacomo Puccini's students, his disciples, exalted in the opportunity to share their Master's life. Let us have the same attitude and never be complacent about serving the Lord. Yes, there will be opposition, but if you live your life as a Christian it should not be easy. We are guaranteed one thing: eternal life will be worth every ounce of our efforts.

Questions to Ponder:

1. What have I done recently to complete Jesus' work in this world?
2. When I am called by the Lord to minister to others, how have I responded?
3. What holds me back from carrying out the mission entrusted by the Lord to his disciples, including Christians today?
4. How have I manifested the person of Jesus to others? What precisely do others see when they observe what I do and hear what I say?
5. How far am I willing to go, moving away from my "comfort zone" to do the Lord's work, to build his Kingdom in our contemporary world?

Be Ready for God's Call

Albert Schweitzer was born to a pious German woman and her Lutheran pastor husband in 1875. With parents of education and raised in a Christian environment, it was not unexpected that he study theology and philosophy at the university. He was a brilliant student and achieved doctorates in both disciplines by the time he had reached his early twenties. As an academic he was well known, especially in his immediate purview of colleagues. In 1910, however, he wrote a book, *The Quest for the Historical Jesus*. This was an effort at using historical criticism in application to the Gospel narratives. The book made him an international celebrity in theology almost overnight.

At the top of his field, one might think it odd to change direction in life. But God called him to do something different, to dedicate himself to music. As a young man, Schweitzer had toyed with the idea of being a professional musician. Now, as he approached the age of 40, he began to tour the major European cities as a concert organist. His interpretation of the music of Johann Sebastian Bach, both on the concert stage and on some of the first phonographic recordings, was unequaled in his day.

After conquering two different disciplines, theology and musical performance, God called Albert Schweitzer again to change directions in his life. This time the shift was a radical step; he was called to become a medical missionary in Africa. The challenge would be great, but he went with confidence that all would be provided. French Equatorial Africa had only been "opened" by Christian missionaries a few decades previously. In the 1920s he established a hospital on the Gonge River in the nation of Gabon. The facility served two functions: as a hospital which met the immediate needs of the local area, and as a leper sanitarium for the greater geographic region. After laboring for more than 30 years in Africa as a doctor, the world in 1952 officially recognized the contribution of Dr. Albert Schweitzer as he was awarded the Nobel Peace Prize. The inscription read, "Granted on behalf of the brotherhood of nations."

Albert Schweitzer accepted several different calls from God. Each required his readiness; each required a certain sense of risk and possibly the need to change. But he went forward, with complete trust, that with God all would be provided.

If God invites, are you ready? This challenging question is posed by Jesus (Matthew 22:1-14). In this parable of the wedding banquet, we hear of God's call, its rejection, and the need to always be ready. In the story we hear that the invitation to the banquet appears to be universal. There are those who are initially invited, the ones who reject the call. There are also those who are called later, those on the highways and along the byroads. We also hear that the call is not a one-time opportunity. Rather, if we at first do not accept God's call, then we can be sure that the call will be extended again and again, for God's call is always present. Some people accept God's call; others reject it. Whether we accept or reject the call to the banquet, however, God's invitation and work will always be present; we may just miss out!

God's call requires our readiness. The parable describes one who, although he accepted the invitation, was not properly dressed, and was dismissed, leading him to be cast into the darkness. The moral of the story is clear: if God calls with an opportunity, we must be ready to respond.

God's call may require us to change; it will involve some risk. In the parable we are told of a farmer and a businessman who were asked to change but could not. If we were to read the Gospel alone then we too might be hesitant to respond, for even one who accepted the invitation but was not properly dressed, was rejected.

God's word, the Scriptures are filled, however, with hope and the ever-abiding presence of God. We may think that the risk is too great, that we cannot take the chance of change. But St. Paul, in writing to the Christian community at Philippi (4:12-20), says that all that is necessary will be provided by God in magnificent ways. Paul knew this reality in his own life. As he says, "I have learned to be content with whatever I have. I know what it is to have little, and I know what it is to have plenty." (11b-12a) Yet, through it all, in Christ he will receive strength for all needs. And if we should wonder or question what will be the providence of God for those of us who take the risk and answer the call, we need look no further than the beautiful metaphors offered by Isaiah 25:6-8. On this mountain the Lord of hosts will make for all peoples a feast of rich food, a feast of well-aged wines, ... And he will destroy on this mountain the shroud that is cast over all peoples, the sheet that is spread over all nations; he will swallow up death forever. Then the Lord God will wipe away the tears from all faces, and the disgrace of his people he will take away from all the earth, for the Lord has spoken." If we can be ready, if we can take the risk and accept the invitation of God, in other words if we can allow God to guide all our decisions, then we will be provided with a richness that God alone can supply.

How is God calling you this day? Possibly God's invitation is in the form of new responsibility, at work, at school, in the community or in the Church. Maybe God's call is in the form of relationship, whether it be friendship, social, romantic or possibly even a renewed relationship with God. Possibly the call from God is to change, to delete something from our ever-busy schedule and to add something new. And if it should be that God is calling us to change must we not ask ourselves the question, what am I willing to take off my slate of things so as to make room for the work of God?

What is God's call for you this day? Each person must answer this question in the privacy of his daily walk and conversation with the Lord in prayer. Albert Schweitzer was called to do many things. Each required his readiness and a certain sense of risk. He responded, however, confident that God's providence would provide all that was necessary. Let us too take the risk; let us jump in. May we accept the loving embrace of God's invitation this day!

Questions to Ponder:

1. Am I "available" to the call of the Lord in my life? Why do I run when God calls me to go in a different direction?
2. What has been my reaction when life has thrown me a "curveball" and I have been forced to proceed in a different direction in life?
3. How is God calling me today? What is he calling me to do that I did not expect?
4. What do I need to do to prepare myself better to accept the call of the Lord in my life?
5. How can I best utilize the gifts and talents given to me to build the Kingdom of God in my world?

Carrying Others' Burdens

     Once in a far-off land there was a great king whose dominion extended far and wide. His power and authority were absolute. One day, as events would happen, a young man, a commoner, committed a grave offense against the king. In response the king and his counselors gathered together to determine what should be done. They decided that since the offense was so grave and had been committed by a commoner against someone as august as the king, the only punishment that would satisfy justice was death. The king's son, the crown prince, however, interceded on the young offender's behalf-- you see they were best friends. The prince spoke with his father and the counselors; the debate grew rather heated. In the end the king declared, "The offender must pay a price for his offense. I decree that he must carry a heavy burden up Temple Mountain. If he survives the ordeal he shall live!"
     The prince again interceded for his friend. He knew the burden of which his father spoke was the weight of death and he knew his friend would not be able to carry it. Thus, the prince declared, "Royal blood has been offended, therefore only royal blood can pay the price." So, the prince shouldered the heavy burden himself, and with his friend trailing behind him, began the ascent of the mountain. The task was very difficult. The higher the prince climbed the heavier the burden became. The prince slipped and stumbled several times, but he always managed to right himself and keep going. When the two friends first saw the summit, their goal, the prince collapsed from sheer exhaustion. He said to his friend, "In order for justice to be served the price must be paid." The young man understood the prince and, thus, he shouldered the burden himself and, now with the prince following, managed to climb the rest of the way to the summit. When the two friends reached their goal, the prince, with his last ounces of strength, lifted the burden high over his head and then he collapsed and died.

The king, observing all these events from below, declared, "Justice has been served, but only for the prince." Then with his great power he returned his son to life. The prince, now returned to life, said, "Not so, not yet. Justice has not been totally served. Royal blood received help along the way!" The king had to agree. Thus, he pardoned the young offender and the two best friends lived happily ever after.

The story, "The Burden: A Tale of Christ," provides an important lesson on the reality of life. We learn that God will always do what God can do in every situation. The Lord will bring the divine presence to any difficulty, shoulder our burdens, and assist us along our way. Equally important, however, is to understand that humans must do their share to help others with their burdens and by this means assist Jesus in the work of salvation. Scripture provides the same lesson.

In Mark's Gospel (1:40-45) Jesus encounters a leper who wishes to be freed of his physical ailment. Jesus also wishes this and thus reaches out, touches the man and he is made clean. In a real way Jesus took on the pain and suffering of the leper--not the physical pain, but the psychological pain of being ostracized, a reality as Jesus broke the laws of purity, making himself unclean. Leviticus 13:45-46a reads, "The person who has the leprous disease shall wear torn clothes and let the hair of his head be disheveled and he shall cover his upper lip and cry out, 'Unclean, unclean.' He shall remain unclean as long as he has the disease; he is unclean." The Book of Leviticus is filled with laws that assisted the Israelites to be faithful to God's commands. In their day these laws were useful, but Jesus clearly moves beyond the law. He reaches out, touches, and heals. In a very real way Jesus lived for others.

I have often asked myself the question--why did Jesus not reach out and cure all the lepers at once. Could he not have gathered all those so afflicted in one place, reached out and cured them all? Could he not have shouldered their burden collectively as the prince shouldered the burden for his commoner friend? Certainly, Jesus did just this when he took upon himself the burden of a sinful world and nailed it to a cross on Calvary. Why then not take on the physical burden as well?

Possibly the answer is because Jesus wanted the Jewish people to do their share to shoulder the burdens of their brothers and sisters. Maybe Jesus wanted his people to reach out and do what they could to assist others. It seems that St. Paul suggested a similar idea when he writes to the Christian community at Corinth: "Be imitators of me, as I am of Christ." (I Corinthians 11:1) Should not the challenge of Jesus and St. Paul to assist others be applied to us today?

The world today is filled with lepers--not those who have the dreaded skin disease (although there are still some of these people), but the many peoples who are treated as lepers by our society. We simply have other names for today's lepers--the poor, the homeless, the physical and mentally handicapped, the immigrant, the prisoner, the sick, the elderly, homosexuals, the lesser educated. The list, unfortunately, could go on. All of these people have generically been placed on the fringes of society. We avoid them and their problems as assuredly as the Jews avoided and placed on the fringes those with leprosy.

The Lord challenges us today to reach out and touch those who are contemporary lepers and assist them with their burdens. Jesus says, help me in my efforts to live for others. As the prince shouldered the burden for his friend, so Jesus tells us to shoulder the burden of those who are less fortunate than ourselves. As we celebrate this Eucharist and are fed by the Body and Blood of the Lord, let us renew our efforts, in mind, soul, and action, to assist those who need us to carry their burdens. Let us do our share to help others. May we participate in the divinity of Jesus, who is our brother, friend, and Lord.

Questions to Ponder:

1. How do I react when I encounter the contemporary lepers in our world? Do I run or minster to them?
2. How do I imitate Christ in my daily life? What do people hear and see in my words and actions?
3. What have I done lately to shoulder the heavy burden that others carry?
4. What more can I do to witness to the power and presence of God in my life?
5. How do I apply the law in my life and others? Where does compassion have a place in my life?

Answering God's Call

One day a holy hermit was walking outside the monastery. He looked about and saw a cripple, a mother begging food for herself and her malnourished child. Additionally, it seemed that both mother and child had been the victims of a severe beating. Seeing them, the holy man turned to God and said, "Great God! How is it that such a loving Creator as you can see so much suffering and yet do nothing about it?" Then deep within his heart the holy monk heard God's reply, "I have done something about it. I made you."

The unexpected answer received by the holy monk, which forced him to ponder his response to God, was experienced by the patriarchs, prophets, and apostles about whom we read in the Scriptures. Imagine the level of faith required by Abram when God commanded him: "Go from your own country and your kindred and your father's house to the land that I will show you. I will make of you a great nation, and I will bless you, and make your name great, so that you will be a blessing." (Genesis 12:1-2) Genesis further tells us that Abram was 75 years old when he left Haran and traveled with his wife and nephew to the land of Canaan. Somehow, without the knowledge of monotheism, Abram believed and set in motion God's plan of Salvation History. God came to Moses in the desert in the form of a burning bush that was not consumed, telling him that he had been chosen to lead the Israelites out of bondage. While Moses was a bit hesitant, he went forward, nonetheless, in obedience to God. His problems and frustrations were numerous, but he always demonstrated fidelity to the call.

The Hebrew prophets were many times not convinced of their call, but nevertheless went forward and responded. Isaiah described himself, "Woe is me! I am lost, for I am a man of unclean lips, and I live among a people of unclean lips." Yet, when the voice of the Lord called, "Whom shall I send, and who will go for us?" he responded, "Here I am; send me." (Isaiah 6:5, 8) Jeremiah had been consecrated from the womb to be a prophet, yet initially balked when asked to prophesy: "Ah, Lord God! Truly I do not know how to speak, for I am only a boy." (Jeremiah 1:6) But the Lord responded, telling him not to be afraid, that he would be with him every step of the way. He then appointed him to proclaim God's message to nations and kingdoms. Amos was a shepherd of Tekoa yet answered the Lord's call by proclaiming a message of social justice to the Northern Kingdom of Israel.

The New Testament, as exemplified by the Apostles and St. Paul, also provides important examples of those who answered the call of God. The Synoptic Gospels tell us that when Jesus called, the apostles responded "immediately," leaving everything and becoming his followers. They had no idea what their positive response would mean for their future lives, but nonetheless they responded in a positive way. The dramatic conversion of St. Paul (Acts 9:1-19) demonstrates the strength of the God's call. Paul, the zealous Pharisee and persecutor of Christians, becomes the great Apostle to the Gentiles, the first great evangelist and one of the greatest sources for Christian theology.

Like the holy hermit, the Hebrew patriarchs and prophets and the apostles of the New Testament, we have been called, through baptism, to live a life of holiness by following the teachings of Jesus Christ. Our call is our vocation. In the past most Catholics equated the word vocation with priesthood and/or religious life, but all people are called to a prophetic vocation, to live their life as mapped out by the great artist God the Father, directed by his Son, Jesus Christ and choreographed by the Holy Spirit. The general vocation for most is to marriage and family, but some are called to the single life and others to the vowed life as a religious.

The call is universal, but particular to each individual. How do we respond to the call of the Lord? Too often we ignore the call; we refuse to acknowledge that God asks us to go in a particular direction. We balk; we close our ears. At times we want to hide or to go in a way 180° opposed to the direction chosen for us by God. Too often as well we prefer the wide, uncluttered, easily trodden and well-worn wide road, the path taken by the majority. Because it is unencumbered, it is a popular route and we will have many companions along way. But as Jesus says in his

Sermon on the Mount, "Enter through the narrow gate; for the gate is wide and the road is easy that leads to destruction, and there are many who take it. For the gate is narrow and the road is hard that leads to life, and there are few who find it."(Matthew 7:13-14)

The extremely busy contemporary world in which we live also impedes our ability to answer freely and fully. We can easily excuse ourselves that one additional thing on our overly busy plate cannot be managed. We shy away from the Lord's call because we feel we are not sufficiently talented, seemingly forgetting that God will provide whatever we need to adequately do the job. At times as well we do not want to get involved and thus, we fail to act.

The immediate and unhesitating response of the apostles to the call of Jesus should be our goal, but even if God must twist an arm a bit, as he did the prophets, answering the Lord's call is what is imperative. We have all been beautifully and uniquely created by God for a purpose that is sometimes obscured, too often by ourselves, but it is unique to us. As the holy hermit was challenged by God to act, rather than complaining to the Lord that nothing had been done, so too must we be open to the call as it is presented to us by God. The well-known Jesuit spiritual writer, John Powell, SJ in his book *Through Seasons of the Heart*, speaks about God's call and our need to respond: "There is an old Christian tradition that God sends each person into this world with a special message to deliver, a special song to sing for others, a special act of love to bestow. No one else can speak my message, can sing my song, or offer my act of love. This is my responsibility; this is entrusted to me."

At times God may call like the crash of the surf on the shore or the power of a hurricane wind, but generally the Lord's call is more subtle, like the quiet whispering sound that spoke to Elijah as he hid in the mountain (I Kings 19:11-13a). Rather than complaining about the world, let us do something about it. Let us answer the call of the Lord this day!

Questions to Ponder:

1. What prevents me from being open to the call of the Lord? Why do I hold back?
2. Why is my trust level in God insufficient to follow the Lord unreservedly?
3. How have I been a vehicle to assist others in answering the call of the Lord in their lives?
4. Why do I at times feel inadequate in my role as a contemporary disciple of Christ?
5. When I have had the courage to venture into unchartered waters in my life, what has been the result? Have I found new avenues in my life in the process?

Commitment to God and God's People

Once there was a monastery in the woods that had fallen upon hard times. In the past it had been a thriving community that was well known and respected throughout the region, but over the last generation the monks had one by one died and there were no new vocations to replace them. The Father Abbot was quite concerned about the future of his monastery, now consisting of himself and three brothers and thus he sought counsel from the local rabbi who was known to be a great sage. The Abbot went to the rabbi and asked him if he had any advice on what to do to save his monastery. The rabbi felt at a loss and said that he too worried about his own congregation; people were too busy and simply were not coming to the synagogue any longer. The two commiserated together and read the Torah. As the Abbot was getting ready to return home the rabbi looked at him and said, "One in your home is the Messiah." The Abbot walked home puzzled as to what the rabbi's words meant.

When he arrived at the monastery the monks asked the Abbot what he had learned. He responded that the rabbi had given him no concrete advice, but he had said in cryptic language, "One in your home is the Messiah." Over the next days and weeks, the monks pondered what this might mean. Was it possible that one of them was the Messiah? If that was the case, then most certainly it was Father Abbot. He had been the leader for more than a generation. On the other hand, it might be Brother Thomas, for he is a holy man and full of light. Certainly, it could not be Brother Eldred. He is old, crotchety and often mean-spirted, but he always seems to be right, regardless of the situation or question. The rabbi could not have meant Brother Phillip. He is very passive--a real nobody, but one must admit that he is always there when someone needs assistance.

As they continued to contemplate this question the old monks began to treat each other with great respect, on the off chance that the one with whom they were dealing really was the Messiah.

Because the monastery was in a beautiful portion of the forest it was common during the spring, summer and fall months for families to come and have picnics on the grounds. During this period people who came seemed to sense the new spirit of respect and love that was present at the Monastery. The people returned often and one day a young man came to the Father Abbot and asked if he could join the community. Soon others inquired and joined and thus after several years the vibrant community at the Monastery was again restored because the wisdom of the rabbi had transformed hearts.

This little story provides an excellent illustration of the need to treat people with respect and be committed to them. God certainly has been committed to humanity since the time of creation. God created the first man, but, as we know from the Book of Genesis, the Lord would not allow him to be alone. No, God created from his own flesh a suitable partner--woman. God's respect for and commitment to humanity reached its apex in Jesus. In the Letter to the Hebrews (2:10) we read how God demonstrated total commitment to us: "It was fitting that God for whom and through whom all things exist, in bringing many children to glory, should make the pioneer of their salvation perfect through suffering." Yes, God sent his son to suffer and die so that we might find life.

As God has demonstrated love, respect, and commitment to us so we must be committed to God through our respect for one another. In the creation story it is implied that God gave the man a suitable partner so that they could be committed to each other. The implicit idea of the Genesis account is made explicit by Jesus when he speaks of the commitment that men and women must make in marriage. We read, "But from the beginning of creation, God made them male and female. For this reason, a man shall leave his father and mother and be joined to his wife, and the two shall become one flesh. Therefore, what God has joined together, let no one separate." (Mark 10:6-9) God gave us one another and we in response must do our best to appreciate those God has given to us.

It is no surprise to anyone that we live in a "throw-away" society. We use paper plates and plastic cups which we toss out when we have used them. Children use disposable diapers and adults use disposable razors. We throw away paper and all sorts of rubbish every day. Although we are getting better as a society in the discipline of ecology, we remain a disposable-oriented population. Therein lies a significant problem. We often treat people as if they are as disposable as the paper plate, razor, or the morning paper.

Our commitment to God can be best lived in our commitment to one another. Relationships are beautiful, but they at times can be troublesome and burdensome. Although some relationships die and others transition from one state to another, we must not reject or discard anyone without our best effort. It is easy today to give up on others because our disposable society makes it appear to be acceptable. Jesus, however, gives us a very different message. Parents cannot give up on the troublesome child simply because drugs, violence, or other inappropriate behavior has strained relationships in the family. Rather, everything must be done to mend the tears and rebuild broken relationships. We cannot give up on the business associate merely because he/she does not come through for us. We cannot give up on best friends, whether they be our neighbors or those who occupy the same house or bed, without our best effort.

The monks in the monastery never realized their problem, namely their lack of respect and commitment to each other, until an outside person, the rabbi, showed them the way and aided their ability to recommit themselves to each other. We may not be so fortunate to have someone from the outside help us. We may have to do most of the work ourselves. But never forget that we have God who is committed to us. Let us recommit ourselves to God by refusing to give up on others. Let us renew our relationships as we continue our journey to God and eternal life.

Questions to Ponder:

1. Why have I at times given up on people, situations or my responsibilities?
2. How respectful am I of others, especially those who might cause me problems or with whom I would not want to share my life?
3. When I have felt rejected by others, what has been my response?
4. What does commitment to others mean to me? How have I manifested my commitment to others?
5. How have I participated, possibly unknowingly, in the "throw-away" society of our contemporary world?

Carrying the Cross of Christ

Agnes Bojaxhiu was a diminutive woman who was ordinary in some ways but extraordinary in all the important avenues of life. She was born on August 26, 1910 in what was then called Macedonia. She was raised by conscientious Catholic parents who taught her the elements of the faith, especially the idea that faith needed to be exercised every day. Agnes began to exercise her faith in a special context at age 18 when she joined the Sisters of Our Lady of Loreto, headquartered in Ireland. After a few months on the Emerald Isle, she was sent by her religious superiors to Darjeeling, India to complete her initial formation. Her first assignment was to teach in a Catholic school in Calcutta. There she experienced the poverty and pain of her students and those who lived in the area.

Agnes taught in the school for several years until something happened that transformed her life. In September 1946, while on a train traveling from Calcutta to Darjeeling, she received a new and powerful call. She realized that she was being called by God to serve the sick, the dying, the hungry, the naked, and the homeless. Her role was to put God's love into action with the poorest of the poor.

Agnes, who had taken the religious name Teresa, did not hesitate or ask questions about her new call. She sought and received permission from Pope Pius XII to leave the Loreto Sisters and start her own congregation. This was the genesis of the Missionaries of Charity, canonically established in 1952, and the start of the famous career of Mother Teresa of Calcutta. Mother Teresa required her sisters to take four vows--the traditional three of poverty, chastity, and obedience, and a fourth, service to the poor, whom she believed embodied Christ on earth. In 1952 she opened Nirmal Hriday (Pure Heart) Home for the dying in Calcutta. This was the first of many such foundations. For the next 45 years Mother Teresa and her community brought the love of God to those who had nothing. The Missionaries of Charity, imitating their master, voluntarily suffer by taking upon themselves the cross of poverty and pain. Over the years, Mother Teresa's organization has grown. Today over 5000 sisters 400 brothers and 40 priests minister as Missionaries of Charity to God's poor in 139 countries.

God's call to the world is to the cross. Our call requires us to act and demonstrate in practice our faith. Mother Teresa, inspired by the Scriptures, knew this all too well. Isaiah 50:4-9, one of the famous "Suffering Servant" passages speaks of one who will suffer, but one who will not rebel and will not turn back. This servant will experience the abuse of the world, but he will not fail. Why? Because God is present and will not allow the servant to be disgraced or be put to shame. God is the help and refuge of those who seek him.

The action of belief was certainly demonstrated by Peter in his famous confession of faith. In responding to Jesus' classic question, "Who do you say that I am," Peter says. "You are the Messiah, the Son of the living God." (Matthew 16: 15-16) Immediately after this proclamation the Lord reveals to his chosen leader what the future will hold, not only for Jesus, but for all who follow in his footsteps. Jesus will suffer and be put to death. We who bear his name may not suffer a physical cross, but we must, as Jesus says, deny ourselves, pick up our cross, and follow his lead. Being a disciple is not easy, but it will lead us home to God. The Lord is ever present and is with us through the ups and downs, the highs and lows, the agonies and the ecstasies of life.

We who follow Jesus, who bear his name, will suffer, if we live our common vocation to holiness well. Life throws us all sorts of twists and turns that may not always take us in the direction we want or bring us the experience we desire. But we must not lose heart. Jesus, the "Suffering Servant" of Isaiah's prophecy, walked a road which brought him much pain. He suffered the emotional trauma of being rejected, especially by his own people and the physical torture of an ignominious death by crucifixion.

How can we transform the Christian vocation to the cross into something that is fulfilling? What will be our response to God's call and to a life that, at times, will bring us suffering? St. James tells us that our response must be to live a life of active faith. Our actions and works demonstrate the faith we possess. As

James writes, "What good is it my brothers and sisters if you have faith but do not have works? ... [F]aith by itself, if it has no works, is dead." (James 2:14a, 17). In other words, faith that is not practiced is thoroughly lifeless.

     How can we manifest our Christian vocation to discipleship, our need to follow Christ and suffer? We do so principally by living for others. Parents live for their children. They sacrifice and deny themselves so that their children may have more. Teachers, physicians, and other professionals live for their students, patients, or other clients. Young people can live for those with whom they associate regularly, whether they are found in the classroom, the playground, or in the family room at home. We must all live for others, not only those we know and like, but possibly more importantly those we do not know or like.

     Mother Teresa of Calcutta became an international celebrity, not because she was rich, powerful, or in possession of great knowledge or personal holdings. She became known worldwide because of her quiet unassuming dedication. She took up the cross of Jesus by helping the poor carry their crosses. She lived an active faith and challenged the world to follow her lead. Let us take up our cross and follow our Master. He did not promise us a rose garden today, but he did promise eternal life tomorrow!

Questions to Ponder:

1. The last time I encountered a "street person" what was my reaction?
2. How do I react to distasteful situations in life? Can I meet such challenges head on or is my reaction less pro-active?
3. What valuable lessons of life have I learned through my own experiences of suffering?
4. When was the last time I spent quality time with a person who was truly in need?
5. What does my common Christian vocation to holiness suggest I must do in serving the poor and those less fortunate in our world?

Service: The Manifestation of God's Care

Once there was a wise, industrious, and generous farmer who had three idle and greedy sons. This farmer was a good person; he was good to those he knew and those he knew not. His goodness shone in his character, even when he experienced pain and difficulty in his life. When the farmer was old and he feared that he would die, he called his sons to his side and gave them his final instructions. He wanted his sons to lead good lives, along the precepts they had been taught in their youth. He concluded saying, "There is a great treasure in a field if you are willing to dig and find it." As soon as the farmer died his greedy sons went to the field and began to dig. They dug from north and south, east and west. They dug up every inch of the field, but they did not find one ounce of gold, silver, or any special treasure. The sons surveyed the field and figured that because their father was a generous man, he might have given the treasure to someone before he died. Before they gave up on the project entirely, however, they decided that since the field was prepared a crop should be sown. They planted wheat and the yield was abundant. After the harvest the wheat was sold, and the sons pocketed a handsome amount of money.

After these events the sons gathered together and began to talk about what they would do with the field. They thought that possibly they had missed the treasure the first time. Thus, they decided to dig it up again. They did the same as before, and obtained the same negative result, but harvested another bumper crop of produce. This process continued for a few years and the sons became acclimated to hard work and the cycle of the seasons, something that was new to them. Over time they also became quite wealthy with the great yield from the field. In the end the sons came to the realization that their father in his instructions so long ago had been training them to work hard and appreciate the value of manual labor. In the process they had become quite wealthy. There really was a great treasure in that field.

This story comes from a collection of tales told by the Sufis, a community of Muslim mystics who lived in the regions of Persia and Turkey many centuries ago. It is certainly a story of how greed is overcome, but more generically it is tale of how good triumphs over evil, how the light transforms the darkness. Scripture describes how the goodness of Jesus triumphed over the evil and darkness of his world and how we are challenged to be servants in order to dispel the darkness and evil we encounter.

The author of the Book of Wisdom (2:12-20) speaks of a good person who is unjustly maligned and violated. We read, "He became to us a reproof of our thoughts, the very sight of him is a burden to us, because his manner of life is unlike that of others." The author continues, "Let us test him with insult and torture, so that we may find out how gentle he is and make trial of his forbearance. Let us condemn him to a shameful death." (Wisdom 2:14-15, 19-20a) The person's whole character is tried. We might ask in response, "Will God be present to those who seek him?"

The answer to this fundamental question of faith is provided by Jesus himself. In Mark 9:30-37 Jesus predicts his own suffering and death. But Jesus will also rise and in so doing will conquer evil and dispel darkness. Will God be present to those who call upon him? The answer is a resounding yes; God is ever present to any and all who seek the Lord.

We live in a world that is at times shrouded in darkness and where evil lives on our front door. We often hear people say, "Why do bad things happen to good people?" The answer many times is human free will. It is through free will that the drunk gets behind the wheel of a car, drives, and in the process kills innocent people. Gangs, like MS-13, using their own free will, arm themselves, roam our streets, spray bullets indiscriminately into a neighborhood, and maim the innocent. Through free will the corrupt politician or civil official pockets the bribe and cheats or swindles others. In the process he destroys not only others, but the very system in which we believe.

God allows our world to operate, both the dynamism of the physical environment and the free will given to each human person. We have a choice; we always have a choice. Often it is our choice if goodness or evil prevails. Thus, we must use our gift of free will wisely. Jesus suggests in the Gospel that the best use of free will is to be a servant. The Lord tells his apostles that the one who wishes to be important must become lowly and be the servant of others. In order to be a servant, we need some assistance along the road. We must seek the wisdom of God to know how best to serve.

If we seek the wisdom of God and if we do our best to be servants then most assuredly God's goodness, manifest in our actions, will triumph and darkness will be dispelled by the light of Christ. God is ever present and thus we know that God always does God's share. We must do our share if God's kingdom is to appear in our midst.

In the Sufi tale the greedy sons, representative of evil, could not overcome the wisdom and goodness of the farmer, even when he was long dead. Similarly, God's goodness will triumph over evil and the light will illumine the darkness of our world, as long as we do our part. Therefore, let us do our best to be servants in order to conquer the evil that we encounter. We do so in imitation of Jesus, who died to set us free and remains our brother, friend, and Lord.

Questions to Ponder:

1. How much am I willing to suffer in order that the message of Jesus can still be proclaimed?
2. Why at times do the allure of power, wealth, and prestige have such a command over what I do?
3. How do I deal with the unexpected events in my life, especially those that cause pain and suffering?
4. When darkness enters the lives of others we know, what has been my response to them? How have I brought them the light?
5. How have I shown the power of God's goodness in my actions towards others?

The Courage to Act

During the 1950s in the American South, segregation was the order of the day. Institutionalized by the infamous 1896 *Plessy vs. Ferguson* decision of the United States Supreme Court, where the doctrine of "separate but equal" became the law of the land, segregation, even in public education, was the scourge of American society. This situation kept the African American community from full equality and thus prevented its members from sharing fully in the American dream.

Segregation was wrong and something needed to be done, but who would have the courage to act? The answer came from an unexpected source in Topeka, Kansas. Oliver Brown and his family lived in Topeka near to a public school. It was totally natural for Mr. Brown to desire that his daughter attend the local school, rather than be bused across town to another institution. There were two problems, however. The Browns were African Americans and the school in their neighborhood was for whites only.

In 1952 Brown, believing the law that prevented his daughter from attending the local school to be unjust, challenged the system. The local and state courts upheld the right of the school to dictate who could attend. Mr. Brown, however, was not to be deterred in his fight for justice. Eventually in 1954 the case was heard by the United States Supreme Court, headed at the time by Chief Justice Earl Warren.

Civil Rights had been a highly volatile ideological issue in the United States since the time of Reconstruction after the Civil War, but Warren was determined to hear the case. The Chief Justice acted with great courage in the face of stiff opposition. He held power and authority and he was determined to use it rightly. Warren possessed sufficient wisdom to realize that such a case would require unanimity; the high court must act without dissension. Thurgood Marshall, the well know civil rights attorney for the NAACP and later a member of the high court himself, argued for the plaintiffs. Distinguished South Carolinian and octogenarian John Davis represented the Topeka Board of Education. Warren engineered the Court's 9-0 unanimous decision in favor of the Brown family. In his written decision the Chief Justice now famously wrote, "In the field of public education, the doctrine of separate but equal has no place. Separate educational facilities are inherently unequal."

It was not easy, and it took much courage, but Earl Warren, possessing authority and power, acted rightly to correct an inherent wrong in American society. Clearly, as presented in the Scriptures, Jesus was one who acted rightly and with courage in his public ministry. We, his followers, are challenged to do the same.

Isaiah was a prophet who wrote to the Hebrew people before, during, and after their exile in Babylon. In the latter third of his long book of prophecy (chapters 56-66), the prophet proclaims that a new day has dawned for the Hebrews. The prophet states, "You shall be a crown of beauty in the hand of the Lord, and a royal diadem in the hand of your God. You shall no more be termed Forsaken and your land shall no more be termed Desolate, but you shall be called My Delight." (Isaiah 62:3-4a) Isaiah was given the gift of prophecy and he knew when and how to exercise it. Now the nation of Israel, recently returned from exile, must have the courage to rebuild its life and to act rightly in response to God's graciousness bestowed on the lives of its people.

The miracle at Cana, when Jesus transformed water into wine is familiar to us all. It was the first great sign of the Lord's public ministry. Jesus was wise; he used a public venue but acted in a private way to demonstrate his power and authority. It is important to note that Jesus did not originally intend to act. Only after Mary, his mother, asked his assistance did he perform the miracle. Jesus knew when to act; he used his judgment properly. In the process he pleased his mother, demonstrated his power, and saved face for the wedding party.

All of us have been given many special gifts with consequent power and authority and we are asked to use them wisely. St. Paul in I Corinthians 12 enumerates some of these gifts: wisdom in discourse, healing, the power to express knowledge, prophecy, tongues, and the interpretation of tongues. How have we used or possibly misused our talents and the authority and power that are derived from them? Power exists in the home. Those who are spouses and parents--do you work as equal partners in your relationship and in the rearing of your children or does one partner dominate the other? Older brothers and sisters--do you act to aid and assist, rather than hurt or ignore your younger siblings? For those who work outside the home and possess a certain amount of power and authority--do you use your talents for the betterment of the company and colleagues as well as your own advancement or does abuse enter, when at times you become too filled with your own self-importance? Those who attend school--if you have great intellectual ability do you use it wisely, study hard, and achieve much? Do you aid those who have lesser ability? Or are you lazy, just getting by, and not working up to your ability? Do we as a community and as individuals have the courage to act when we perceive a wrong exists? Are we lazy, tired, or too busy to right the evils we see? Do we use the gifts we possess--speech, listening, teaching, technical skills--and the authority and power derived from them rightly? Are we building society and thereby the Kingdom of God or are we apathetic and frozen in a world of inaction?

    We have all been given gifts and opportunities to use them wisely--how have we faired? In 1954 Earl Warren had the courage to act and right an inherent wrong in American society. Many thought he was wrong; many more knew he was right but did not possess the courage to act. Jesus had power and he knew when and how to act so as to bring people closer to God. Let us think about our individual situations and determine when and how we will act. Let us have courage and be firm in our resolve to act rightly. It is the Lord whom we follow, it is he who will assist us--today and to eternal life!

Questions to Ponder:

1. When was the last time I acted with courage to right a wrong that I observed?
2. Where do I go and whose counsel do I seek when things are not going well? What is my trust level in God?
3. In what capacity do I use the gifts, talents, time and opportunities that come my way? Who benefits from my efforts?
4. How do I utilize the power and authority I possess? Why at times do I abuse these special gifts from God?
5. When placed in a position to do "the right thing" rather than follow the crowd, what has been my response?

Responding Daily to God's Call

Alfred Bessette was born in August 1845 in the province of Quebec, Canada, the eighth of twelve children. From the outset his life would be one of challenge and response. The first great challenge came in the form of precarious health. Alfred was baptized immediately after he was born so fearful was the attending doctor that he would die. Poor health continued to plague him throughout his youth. He was not able to play and enter into the normal activities of a child, but rather spent his time doing other things, many times working to help support the family because they were so poor. Because Alfred was working, he did not have the advantage of much formal education.

Challenges continued to come his way as the years passed. When he was twelve, he was orphaned. He went to live with relatives for a couple of years, but then he became a migrant laborer traveling throughout Quebec and Ontario and even into the northern New England States.

When Alfred was 22, he answered another call. It seems that God had been tugging on him for a few years to look at religious life as his ultimate vocation. After some investigation, Alfred joined the Brothers of Holy Cross, known originally as the Brothers of St. Joseph from their origins in France. In 1870 he received the habit and was given the religious name Andre. He was sent to the College de Notre Dame in Montreal as a porter, a common doorman. Each day Brother Andre would open the door and greet visitors. It was a repetitive, boring, and mundane job, but it was his responsibility and Andre did his best to respond to the challenge. Andre had special gifts, however, which God would soon reveal.

As he would greet people at Notre Dame many visitors told Andre of friends and family who were sick. After his duties at the College ended each day, Andre would go and visit the sick. He brought with him oil which burned in a sanctuary lamp beside a statue of St. Joseph, the Brothers' patron. When Andre applied the oil to those who were sick many were healed. Soon word of Brother Andre's ability to heal circulated throughout the region. People came from all around to seek Andre's intercession and aid. The sheer number of people, plus the fact that many who came had infectious and contagious diseases, worried many, including Andre's religious superiors, who forbade him from receiving the sick. Andre obeyed; it was another way for him to respond to the challenge of God.

The sick, however, continued to come. A compromise was struck whereby Andre was given permission to set up a small shelter across the street from the College where he could receive the sick. Each day, after his duties as porter were concluded, he would cross the street and spend many hours, sometimes until late at night speaking with those who stood in line for their turn to speak to this humble and saintly man. Opposition continued to come, however. Diocesan officials were concerned about what was happening and local doctors thought Andre to be some kind of quack. Through it all Andre continued to answer the call and to carry out his responsibilities as best he could.

In 1909 the Holy Cross community obtained a large piece of land in Montreal upon which to build a church in honor of St. Joseph. When a temporary structure was constructed Andre was sent there to continue his duties as porter. For 25 years he opened the door and greeted visitors and for an equal amount of time he continued to work miraculous cures. People came from all around to meet Andre. Many were cured but many more were converted by the faith he exhibited and the ability to respond to God, as shown by this humble servant of God. God's call came to Andre each day, but it was always packaged in different ways. Sometimes it was the simplicity of opening a door and other times it was the miracle of healing. Each time Brother Andre answered the call.

The story of Brother Andre Bessette, whose simple life of humble service eventually led to his canonization by Pope Benedict XVI in 2010, encourages us who receive God's daily challenges to respond in love.

Jeremiah was a reluctant prophet. Like some of his stripe he did not want the job, but he writes, "Before I formed you in the womb I knew you, and before you were born I consecrated you; I appointed you a prophet to the nations." (Jeremiah 1:5) Jeremiah's ministry would not be easy, but God would provide him with all that was necessary to carry out the task. There would be opposition, but the antagonism would not prevail. Jeremiah answered the call and spoke God's words to the Hebrew people, but they were not willing to listen. The failure of the people to heed God's message, to carry out the responsibilities of the covenant which God had revealed to Moses on Mount Sinai, resulted in their exile from the land of Israel.

Similarly, Jesus' ministry was not easy. He proclaimed harsh and difficult words that raised eyebrows and challenged many. At the outset the people were favorable to Jesus' challenge. St. Luke (4:22) writes, "All spoke well of him and were amazed at the gracious words that came from his mouth." But when Jesus went further and reminded the people of their past failures, during the times of Elijah and Elisha, to respond to the challenge of God, they became indignant, expelled him from the city and intended to hurl him from the cliff. As with Jeremiah, Jesus was challenging the Hebrews of his day to respond to God's call.

God calls each of us on a daily basis to respond to the many challenges of life. What has been our record to date? One might ask - what is the common call to which all who bear the name Christian are to respond? The answer is our common vocation to holiness, articulated by Jesus as the Golden Rule--to love God and love our neighbor as our self. Contemporary prophets speak this message to us, but are we listening? The challenges that come our way may be significant and ask us to do things and make decisions that influence many others. Most of the time, however, our daily responsibilities are repetitive, simple, and mundane. Brother Andre opened the door and he healed, but in both the simple and the spectacular he answered the call.

All of us have been called to respond. Parents receive the daily call to respond to their children's daily needs. What parents do is not generally material for the front page of the papers, but it may be the most important task they will ever have. Spouses must respond to each other with truth and sensitivity. Working people are certainly tasked with many responsibilities, but whether the responsibility be great or small, the challenge is the same. Young people also have the need to answer God's call through their responsibilities in the classroom, athletic field, clubs and organizations, and maybe most importantly their duties with family and God.

    Brother Andre faced many challenges, but he always responded with the spirit of love which Paul describes in the famous passage from I Corinthians 12:31-13:13. Let us face our challenges and not shy away. We do so in imitation of Jesus, our brother, friend and Lord.

Questions to Ponder:

1. How have I reacted when someone challenged me to do more, to answer the call with greater vigor?
2. What daily tasks can I make more significant by placing God at the center of my actions?
3. Why at times do I run from the challenge that God sends my way? What is my fear?
4. How can I be more cooperative with God's will in my life?
5. Why at times do I believe that I have no responsibility in the work of building God's Kingdom in our world?

Serve God Willingly

In the seventh year of his reign, two days before his 65th birthday, before a full consistory of cardinals, Jean Marie Barette, Pope Gregory XVII, signed an instrument of resignation, took off the Fisherman's ring, handed his seal to the Cardinal Camerlengo and made a curt speech of farewell. So begins the powerful tale of courage and faith, *The Clowns of God*, by Morris West, the famous Australian novelist.

In the story the Pope has seen a vision of the Second Coming. He thinks it imperative that the message of the vision be communicated to the whole world. He goes, therefore, to seek advice from his chief counselors, the Curia and the College of Cardinals. They are unimpressed. It will ruin our work they claim. The whole world will be thrown into a panic. You cannot promulgate such a message. The Pope feels frustrated; what is he to do? He is tired of the arrogance of his advisors. In order to be true to himself and God, he believes the only viable option is to resign. Therefore, he leaves Rome and places himself under obedience to a Benedictine abbot in a small monastery outside the eternal city. There he will contemplate his future.

One week later, alone and without support, the former pope receives his first visitor. The visitor is Carl Mendelius, a longtime friend and former Jesuit priest who is now teaching theology as a layman at a prestigious German university. Together the two friends plan how the important message of Jean Marie's vision can be promulgated. They are sure about one thing - whatever message is released must be unpretentious, simple and undramatic so that all may understand and prepare themselves for the Lord's return.

Unfortunately, the plans of the two men are foiled; the message is never published. As Mendelius prepares to post a joint statement written by the two men about the vision, and addressed to people throughout the world, he is killed by a bomb planted by an assassin. Jean Marie himself suffers a severe heart attack as he waits to give a speech to a group in England announcing the same statement.

As Jean Marie clings to life in a London hospital he receives a visitor. The man appears to be in his mid-30s; he says that he comes from the Middle East. He wears a very old ring with the ancient Christian symbol of the fish etched on its top. The stranger, who calls himself Mr. Atha, tells the former pope that the message of the vision is important, but that he will be shown that the essential message given is already being lived in the world.

Several weeks later, after Jean Marie has recovered sufficiently to leave the hospital, he returns to his native land of France to fully recuperate. One day he is strolling in a Parisian park. He happens along a group of children. These are special children; they are mentally handicapped. He sits down on a bench and observes these children who are totally unassuming. They live each day as God gave it to them. They are without pretension. In a special way these children serve God. These children, who Jean Marie calls the "Clowns of God." somehow know that the ultimate justice of God, God's return to the world, is already present with them. These children have the goodness, love and generosity of God all wrapped up in them right now. The message of Mr. Atha now begins to make sense to Jean Marie. These children are already living the essential message of the vision, preparedness for God. The world only needs to be able to see and recognize it.

At the end of the novel Jean Marie and his adopted friends, the "Clowns of God" are together in a cabin on a snowy French mountainside. They have gathered to celebrate the Christmas feast. To this out of the way place Mr. Atha arrives quite unexpectedly. He has come to claim his own. Yes, Jesus, the Christ, has seen through all the pretensions of society and has come to claim the world.

Morris West's novel says that those without pretension, those who are willing to live simply, serving God today, will have God return to them. In a similar way Scripture powerfully and beautifully tells us that those who live in God's presence will in the end find God as well.

In Luke's Gospel (18:9-14) Jesus contrasts the approach of two men who go to the Temple to pray, using very different approaches. The first method is that of the Pharisee. From all outward indications the Pharisee does not appear to be a bad person. After all, he says that he has kept all the dictates of the law of the Lord. The problem, however, with the Pharisee is that his attitude, his way of doing things, is all wrong. The Pharisee places himself above all others. He is not content to remain unnoticed, to simply live his life today. Like the Cardinals in Morris West's novel the Pharisee must retain control and position in his life.

The other approach to God is that of the Tax Collector. The Tax Collector is a broken person and knows it. He is not interested in a name or position. He simply wants to live in God's presence in the way that God gives him to live this day. The Tax Collector chooses to quietly go about his business and allow the just God to observe and judge.

When we hear such a Gospel, we might ask ourselves, to whom does God listen when we lift our voices in prayer? Scripture gives us the answer to this important question as well. Sirach (35:16-17), part of the Wisdom literature of the Hebrew Bible, reads, "He [God] will not show partiality to the poor, but will listen to the one who is wronged. He will not ignore the supplication of the orphan or the widow when he pours out his complaint." In other words, God listens to the weak, the orphan, the poor, the anawim, and to the Clowns of God. Importantly, however, we are also told that God is a God of justice; God plays no favorites. Thus, most assuredly, the sincere prayer of all who lift themselves to God will be heard.

How do we approach God in our daily prayer, our day-to-day effort to live the Christian life? Some of us live as the Tax Collector, the *anawim*, the poor, the "Clowns of God." Some of us live with more self-righteousness as did the Pharisee. Our status may change in our life, over a long period of time or, through some windfall or failure, overnight. We may be well known or unknown, or for most of us somewhere in the middle between the maximum and minimum of fame. Wherever we find ourselves the question needs to be asked: Can we willingly live today in the presence of the Lord, or are we constantly fighting God? Can we simply live or is it necessary that God and others know what we have done? Can we believe that God can see through all the pretension, all the smoke and haze of our society and look to the heart? Can we believe that God sees us and accepts us as we are, with our brokenness, our inadequacies, our frailties? We certainly can and should extoll ourselves and others when we can, but we need not make ourselves self-important as did the Pharisee. Rather, we need to live today in God's presence whether we are married or single, well known or unknown, rich or poor. If we can live in God's presence, then the just God will certainly hear our prayer and the goodness we aim to express.

In Morris West's novel the Pope sees a vision of the Second Coming. Over time he comes to realize that the essential message of that vision, readiness for God's return, is already being lived out by some if we can only open our eyes and see it. Let us, therefore, do our best to simply live in God's presence, trusting that the Lord will guide us every step of the way.

Questions to Ponder:

1. Why am I too often preoccupied with the concerns of the future and cannot live in the moment of the day?
2. Why do I sometimes feel I need to impress God and others about my self-importance?
3. Why do I sometimes give up on my prayer, believing that God is not listening or does not care?
4. What can I do to raise up those who are the *anawim* of contemporary life, allowing them to appreciate their inherent human dignity?
5. What can I do to avoid contemporary society's trap to live the self-importance demonstrated by the Pharisee?

A Good Tree is Known by its Fruits

A man owned a magic opal ring. Anyone who wore it became so good that everyone respected and loved the person. Before he died, the man gave each of his sons an opal ring. After their father died, the sons quarreled among themselves about which of them had the magic ring. In order to settle the dispute, they went to an old man who was known to be a great sage. "My sons," said the old man, "only time will show which of you has the magic ring. How you live your lives will show which of you has the magic ring."

There is a story told of a young missionary who spotted a woodcutter at work in the forest. He had heard about this man before and realized that he had never heard of Jesus. "What a perfect opportunity," thought the missionary, "to make a convert for the Lord." All day long the man chopped wood, carried it to his wagon and then walked back to chop another load. All the while the missionary was telling the man about Jesus. At the end of the day the missionary asked, "Well are you ready to accept Jesus Christ?" The woodcutter answered, "I don't know. All day long you have been telling me about how this Jesus was a man who helped others with their burdens, yet you have never helped me with mine."

One day a woman made an interesting discovery. She went to her basement seeking some potatoes for a stew she planned to prepare. The potatoes were kept in the darkest corner of the room. She noticed when she went to that corner some of the potatoes had sprouted and she wondered how they had received the light to grow. Then all of a sudden, a bright ray of light struck her face. The light from the window had hit a highly polished copper kettle that reflected the light onto the potatoes. The woman was excited about her discovery and exclaimed, "I may not be a preacher or a teacher with the ability to expound on the Scriptures, but at least I can be a copper kettle Christian, catching the rays of the Son of God and reflecting that light to someone living in a dark corner."

These three vignettes have, I believe one common message--what we do and the example we set is of vital importance in our lives. Scripture on numerous occasions describes the importance of example, telling us that we will know a good tree by the fruit it bears.

The Book of Sirach is one of the great treasures in the Roman Catholic canon of Scripture, part of Wisdom Literature and also the apocrypha, the seven books in the Old Testament viewed by Catholics as part of the canon (making a total of 46 Old Testament books). The book is filled with many proverbs and important lessons on how to properly live one's life in this world. Sirach (27:4-7) tells us that what a person says is of great importance for it is through one's speech that a person is tested and found to possess wisdom. A person's words tell us a lot about an individual. They tell us not only that one might be well educated, but more profoundly the attitude that one possesses. Through a person's words we can know if that one prefers conciliation or revenge, love or hate, compassion or anger, and humility or arrogance.

In a similar way, St. Luke's Gospel (6:39-45) uses several images that emphasize the importance of leading lives that others would wish to emulate. We often make judgments about people that make them appear to be less important than ourselves. Jesus says, "Why do you see the speck in your neighbor's eye, but do not notice the log in your own?" (6:41) Sometimes we convince ourselves into believing that nothing could possibly be wrong with us. The problem is always "out there" with others. Jesus goes on to say, "No good tree bears bad fruit, nor again does a bad tree bear good fruit." (6:43) We are never neutral on others. Either we are attracted to or pushed away from others; there is no in-between position. If we have goodness in our heart than the fruits of that goodness will be manifest in how we act toward and speak about others.

Setting a good example in our actions and words is not always easy. In fact, it is often quite difficult. The challenge is met by St. Paul who says when we are fully engaged in the work of the Lord, we must strive to show the face of God to others in our daily lives. He writes to the Corinthians, "Therefore, my beloved, be steadfast, immovable, always excelling in the work of the Lord, because you know that in the Lord your labor is not in vain." (I Corinthians 15:58) At home we must be the Christ to others. Parents have the grave responsibility to always speak and act in ways that would make their children proud. Mothers and fathers are the first teachers of their children in everything and children will model the behavior they observe. Children have a special responsibility. Older children must help those who are younger and although it may surprise us at times, the younger ones often put the older ones to shame by the way they speak and act. In the workplace we also need to demonstrate the proper example. If our work ethic is immoral, if we accomplish goals without regard to the needs or feelings of others then that is the way the company will operate. If we treat our co-workers with respect, we might be amazed at their positive response.

The sons who possessed the opal rings, the missionary and the copper-kettle Christian learned the importance of demonstrating good example in varied ways. Jesus has given us the perfect example to follow. He chose to be one like us in all things but sin so that he could show us the way. What we seek is eternal life and the way we achieve it is the example we set. A little story illustrates our challenge.

A rich man had a dream in which he died and went to heaven. St. Peter was escorting him down a lovely street on which each house was magnificent. The man pointed out one especially beautiful home to St. Peter who said, "That is the house of one of your servants." "Well," said the man, "if my servant has a house like that, I can't imagine the magnificent mansion I will occupy." After some time, they came to another street where the houses were very tiny. "You will live in that hut," said St. Peter pointing his finger. "Me, live in such a hovel," said the man in anger. "This is the best we can do for you," said St. Peter. "You must understand that we only build your home up here with the materials of good works and proper example that you sent ahead when you were still on earth." Let us follow the example of the copper-kettle Christian and shine the light of Christ on others by what we do and say and, in the process, move closer to God and eternal life.

Let us today live in the presence of God. Let us embrace the simple approach. Let us willingly serve God without pretension. If we can then certainly God will hear us; God will come. God will claim us as his own in the heavenly banquet of eternal life.

Questions to Ponder:

1. Through my example, as a parent and/or mentor, have I given children and others in my charge the correct message?
2. How do I treat others in my day-to-day life?
3. If I had to answer today what type of house would I occupy in heaven, what would it be?
4. How can I be a "copper-kettle Christian" in my daily life? What needs to change to make this a reality?
5. What have I done lately to lift the burdens of contemporary life from one in distress?

The Hunger for Justice

"Free at last, free at last - thank God Almighty, we are free at last." Those words were spoken by Martin Luther King, Jr. when he concluded his famous "I Have a Dream" speech. This famous address, proclaimed on the steps of the Lincoln Memorial during the March on Washington in August 1963, demonstrated that Dr. King was a man who lived for and, through his work, fed the hunger of his people for justice.

Martin Luther King, Jr. was born in Atlanta, Georgia on January 15, 1929. He followed the path of his father and became a Baptist minister, serving the needs of his people. Along the road he graduated from Morehead College in 1948 and eventually achieved a doctorate from Boston University in 1955. While a graduate student, he met and married Coretta Scott.

The rocky road of service that King traveled began rather harmlessly. Leaving Boston, he settled in Montgomery, Alabama and became the pastor of Dexter Avenue Baptist Church. All was normal, settled, and calm until on December 1, 1955 Rosa Parks, a young African American woman, refused to move to the back of a Montgomery city bus. The event changed Martin Luther King; it changed the history of the United States. King became the leader of a boycott of the Montgomery transportation system. He saw the injustice that had been perpetrated; he met the need!

The course of Dr. King's career as leader of the American Civil Rights movement was now set in motion. For the next thirteen years he would travel about the nation on a campaign to bring justice and to feed the needs of his people. In 1960 he returned to his native city of Atlanta as pastor of his father's former parish, Ebenezer Baptist Church. Along the road of justice, he was many times incarcerated. While in the Birmingham city jail in 1963, he wrote, without the aid of any outside sources, his famous "Letter from a Birmingham Jail," which is considered a masterpiece of contemporary theological thought. Later that same year he led the aforementioned March on Washington. In 1964 he was awarded the Nobel Peace Prize for his efforts to bring justice to Black Americans. He led drives for better housing in Chicago and racial justice in Selma, Alabama. In April 1968 he came to Memphis, Tennessee to lead a strike by the city's sanitation workers. There on April 4 an assassin's bullet ended Dr. King's life and his campaign for justice; he was only 39 years old. In his relatively short life, he had fed the hunger of his people for the justice they deserved.

    Scripture describes how God feeds the hunger of his people in so many ways. Elisha was a prophet who fed the Hebrews with God's word but also physically. In an encounter with a man from Baal-shalishah (II Kings 4:42-44), Elisha miraculously feeds 100 people with 20 barley loaves. It did not seem that there would be enough food; the human perspective saw no possibility. But through the power of God, Elisha was not only able to provide what was needed, there was an excess as well. It was a miracle. God provided for the needs of the people; their hunger was fed that day. Chapter 6 of John's Gospel shows Jesus feeding the people, both physically and spiritually. In John 6:1-15 Jesus provides for the immediate needs of the people; he gives them their daily meal. Jesus multiplies the loaves and fish; he personally distributes the food to each person. In this way he nourishes the people and provides for their bodily needs. But Jesus does more than simply provide physical food. He teaches the people that God will provide in abundance. Nothing must go to waste; all must be used for God's work and greater glory. Later in John 6:22-59 Jesus preaches his famous "Bread of Life" discourse, describing how he will provide himself as the spiritual food the people need to "consume" in order to find life eternal.

    God will provide for our hungers as well. We need, however, to ask, "What is it that our world needs; for what do we hunger?" Certainly, the world hungers for food. Fifty percent of the world's people go to bed hungry each night. The world also hungers for peace. Daily events in many war-torn places demonstrate the great need for God's words of peace. We hunger for love. The world is filled with broken families and spousal abuse; crime and drugs threaten to dominate society while providing an enticing alternative for many, especially our youth.

The world also continues to hunger for justice. Possibly this is the principal hunger of our world. We hunger for decency and respect; we hunger for human justice that all people, created in the image and likeness of God, should enjoy. The world's peoples and nations cry out for justice. Racial tensions and violence are a constant threat to civil tranquility. Religious injustice, although not as evident in the United States, exists here as well as many events do not make the front page of the newspapers. Sex discrimination lowers the dignity of women, objectifies their being, and refuses to respect their equal contribution to society. Political injustice is also present in the demagoguery found in dictatorships and, on a local level, the trash campaign styles which now dominate the American political scene.

Jesus is the answer to all the hungers of our world, but as St. Teresa of Avila has written, since Jesus is no longer physically present, we are the hands, the feet, and the eyes of the Lord in our world. Thus, it is through our efforts that the hungry must be fed. It is through our work that the world can know peace. Justice and a spirit of love are brought to the world by our ministry and example. Our efforts are the endeavors of God; God works through us.

Martin Luther King, Jr. saw the hunger which existed for his people. They hungered for their human rights; they hungered for justice. Dr. King led the campaign which aimed to provide Black Americans with the respect and rights they deserved as children of God. Jesus provides for us as well on a daily basis. He feeds us with the fruits of this earth; he provides us with the Bread of Life. Jesus brings justice to all people and all situations through his omnipresent love. We, as the presence of Christ in our world, are asked to provide for others, to meet the hunger, the need, of those we encounter. Let us always remember our responsibility as stated well by Amnesty International, "Give bread to the hungry and to those who have bread, a hunger for justice."

Questions to Ponder:

1. What can I do to satisfy the cry of the poor and the hunger for justice in our world?
2. How have I satisfied the hunger for Christ that is so evident in our world?
3. When was the last time I took the opportunity afforded me to make a difference in someone's life?
4. When I have felt a "hunger" in my life, for things, people, success, where have I gone for answers?
5. When I have observed or experienced injustice what has been my reaction and how have I responded?

Afterword

The Christian journey is marked by three significant and continuous paths, those of faith, discipleship, and ministry. The journey begins with developing our life of faith, a process initiated, whether we knew it or not, at our baptism and continues throughout our life, growing day-by-day. When we have sufficient maturity in faith, we progress to our life of discipleship. This step requires us to make a commitment to the Lord, to agree to walk in his footsteps as did those he first called to be his disciples, and then the many who have followed over the two millennia of Christian history. Once we have made the commitment to be disciples, then we must manifest this allegiance by acting on the faith we have been given and the discipleship we have freely chosen.

Hopefully, the journey you have just taken through this book has given you much to ponder and consider, as well as bringing challenges in the areas of faith, discipleship, and ministry. It is my hope as well that the personal challenges found herein can assist you in understanding and advancing your life as a person of faith, who seeks through fidelity to discipleship to do what you can, using your God-given abilities and the opportunities that come my way, to help build the Kingdom of God in our world. Christianity is indeed a great privilege, but with all great privileges comes significant responsibility. While we might not be able to individually generate systemic change in our society or change drastically the direction of world events or the path of the Church, we can and must do what we can. As the expression goes, "Think globally, but act locally." All our endeavors, if engaged with the proper attitude and an openness to possibilities, can be transformative on the micro-level and add, day-by-day, to the conversion of our world. We must all continue to walk the road doing our part; God will surely do the rest!

The Christian Journey to Jesus Through Stories

Faith, Discipleship and Ministry

www.ingramcontent.com/pod-product-compliance
Lightning Source LLC
Chambersburg PA
CBHW030151100526
44592CB00009B/221